Honey West

by John C. Fredriksen

Honey West
© 2009 John C. Fredriksen. All Rights Reserved.

All illustrations are copyright of their respective owners, and are also reproduced here in the spirit of publicity. Whilst we have made every effort to acknowledge specific credits whenever possible, we apologize for any omissions, and will undertake every effort to make any appropriate changes in future editions of this book if necessary.

No part of this book may be reproduced in any form or by any means, electronic, mechanical, digital, photocopying or recording, except for the inclusion in a review, without permission in writing from the publisher.

Published in the USA by:
BearManor Media
P O Box 71426
Albany, Georgia 31708
www.bearmanormedia.com

ISBN 1-59393-346-0

Printed in the United States of America.

Book & cover design by Darlene Swanson of Van-garde Imagery, Inc.

To the cast and crew of *Honey West*

Contents

Reflections on a Sylphic Sleuth 1

Gloria Fickling 13

Anne Francis 23

John Ericson 33

Gene LeBell 43

Irene Hervey 57

Sharon Lucas 61

Bruce the Ocelot 65

A. C. Shelby Cobra 289 69

Synopses 73
    "Who Killed the Jackpot?" 73
    "The Swingin' Mrs. Jones" 79
    "The Owl and the Eye" 83
    "The Abominable Snowman" 87
    "A Matter of Wife and Death" 91
    "Live a Little...Kill a Little" 95

"Whatever Lola Wants..." 101
"The Princess and the Paupers" 105
"In the Bag". 111
"The Flame and the Pussycat" 115
"A Neat Little Package". 119
"A Stitch in Crime" 123
"A Million Bucks in Anybody's Language" 127
"The Grey Lady" 133
"Invitation to Limbo". 137
"Rockabye the Hard Way" 141
"A Nice Little Till to Tap" 145
"How Brillig O, Beamish Boy" 149
"King of the Mountain" 153
"It's Earlier Than You Think" 157
"The Perfect Un-Crime" 161
"Like Visions and Omens...and All That Jazz" . . . 165
"Don't Look Now, But Isn't That Me?" 169
"Come to Me, My Litigation Baby" 173
"Slay, Gypsy, Slay" 177
"The Fun-Fun Killer" 181
"Pop Goes the Easel" 185
"Little Green Robin Hood" 189
"Just the Bear Facts, Ma'am". 193
"There's a Long, Long Fuse a' Burning" 197
"An Eerie, Airy Thing" 201

Appendix. 205

Footnotes. 213

Anne Francis horsing around on the set of Honey West; who said 18-hour days cannot be fun?

Reflections on a Sylphic Sleuth

CIVILIZATION, SELDOM STATIC, is for the most part dynamic and constantly evolving. In fact, change is the common denominator of human existence and lucky for us; were it otherwise we may have never ventured beyond caves. Within my own lifetime some of the biggest changes wrought have been those respecting the role of women in society, what they can and cannot do, and the gradual–if grudging–acceptance of said changes by the male of the species. Casting a long glance back through history, this was no mean feat: down through the ages the vast majority of females were condemned by custom or ignorance to closely prescribed roles as wives and mothers, with little toleration for deviations from the norm. Witness the continuing plight of women in certain parts of the Muslim world, whose treatment of them can only be described as medieval, if not outright oppressive. We in the West also exhibited little enlightenment regarding women for centuries but, in the United States at least, attitudes toward traditional roles began breaking down by the late 1950s. The burgeoning middle class arising after World War II, with its concomitant increase and wealth and opportunities for social mobility, stimulated the growth of a restless youth culture-rock 'n' roll, teen flicks, Elvis movies, and make-out pits (drive-ins). Briefly put, adolescent rebellion had gone mainstream and groomed profound questioning of traditional values and social mores by an entire generation of young people. The sexual revolution, then in its infancy, also held the promise of greater self-identity and personal choices for both genders. During early years of the 1960s, this social trend was aided and abetted by popular media, commencing with sexually liberating James Bond films in which women were not simply viewed as sexual objects (a hallmark of the genre), but as capable agents and adversaries. Such portrayals mark a far cry from the orderly media matrons of 1950s television and movies, best typified by June Cleaver and shows like *Father Knows Best*. This decade was a period of cultural conformity and consensus, so the use of media to consciously parrot and reinforce such norms is hardly surprising. However, the overwhelmingly popular response to Bond films, 1962-1965, suggests that younger members of American society were readily receptive to change. Consequently, embedded social taboos respecting female freedom and empowerment began tumbling to the wayside, albeit in due course.

In its own peculiar way, *Honey West* was part of that trend and played a small but significant role in elevating female stereotypes through the broadcast milieu. This was the first American, prime-time television show with the audacity to suggest, even celebrate, a reality that gender was no obstacle to attainment. Moreover, its failure as a series was due entirely to business, not social, considerations and the gauntlet was quickly picked up by another trend-setting show, *The Avengers*. Still, its broadcast significance emanates from being the first American detective series whereby the central role was carried by a woman.[1] In penning this book, I hope to call to the attention of posterity a relatively minor program in industry terms, but one wielding indelible impact on those recalling it through the prism of youth and wonderment. This endeavor is also, in essence, a primer for *Honey West*, a brief reintroduction paving the way for more detailed studies to follow.

The character Honey West originated in the fertile imagination of Forrest "Skip" Fickling (1925-1998), a California advertising and publicity director. She was envisioned by him as a sexy female private eye, a cross-pollinization of Marilyn Monroe and Mike Hammer, a woman who invariably solved her cases and shed her clothes while disposing of criminal elements. Commencing in 1957 with *This Girl for Hire*, Skip, in concert with his wife Gloria, penned eleven Honey West novels under the pseudonym G. G. Fickling. These were all rather formulaic in the pulpy sense with strong sexual overtones, even by the standards of the genre. Honey, however, resonated strongly with the low-brow crowd; her eleven novels were translated into nine languages, and sold seven million copies world-wide. The resulting windfall enabled Skip and Gloria to purchase a tony abode overlooking exclusive Laguna Beach which they touted as "The House that Honey West Built."

Enter Aaron Spelling, the legendary progenitor and producer of some of the worst and most popular successful TV programming in American broadcast history.[2] In 1964 Spelling visited England while working for Four Star Productions and there espied an early *Avengers* episode with noted blonde actress Honor Blackman in the role of special agent Cathy Gale. Blackman, clad in tight leather garments and routinely roughing up male adversaries with martial arts, simply fired up Spelling's imagination. Seeking an American counterpart, he apparently offered Blackman the role of Honey West, but she declined in order to appear as Pussy Galore in the latest Bond venture, *Goldfinger* (1965). Undaunted, Spelling started casting his net about Hollywood and settled upon Anne Francis, another striking blonde known for fetching good looks and acting ability.

Lacking the time to produce a pilot, he introduced Honey West in an episode of his successful series *Burke's Law* entitled "Who Killed the Jackpot," broadcast on April 21, 1965. The script was a collaboration between the husband-and-wife team of Paul Dubov and Gwen Bagni, who would figure prominently in the subsequent series. Anne handled her execution of Honey with panache and even managed to outfox Gene Barry's formidable investigator in a daunting game of

The fantastic stunt woman Sharon Lucas in the climactic fight scene of the Honey West pilot, The Gray Lady.

cat-and-mouse. The show received excellent ratings for that evening and favorable commentary afterwards, so Spelling took matters to the next level by promoting Honey for her own show. Cognizant of Hollywood's well-known attitude toward women, he tailored his pitch accordingly–and had no problem selling the concept. "We met with ABC to tell them our idea about this sexy female private detective, and I had Nolan Miller draw sketches of this slinky, beautiful Honey for them," Spelling recalled. "In one she carried a whip and the other she was sitting with a tiger. 'And that,' I said, 'is the show.' Like James Bond it was based on a series of books and ABC bought it immediately."[3] In Tinseltown, as in life, one goes with what works.

As a show, *Honey West* proved less earth-shattering than groundbreaking, being the first American TV program with a female lead completely in charge of her job–and herself. Some threads of continuity with the novels still manifested: Honey remains a "private eyeful" and a crack investigator who inherited her father's agency after he died. She is also still flippant and quick with her wits–and her fists. This time, however, Honey is more disposed toward keeping her wardrobe on and the series had been sanitized of any references to the tawdry, borderline titillation that was the hallmark of the Ficklings' books. Anne Francis was also magnificently attired with tres chic attire that set the studio back $50,000–a hefty sum in those days. Foremost among her many costumes was a memorable, skin-tight black catsuit artfully clinging to every curve, and which she invariably donned while "catting around" at night. Yet, while the central character exudes tremendous sex appeal (and no one questions Anne Francis as a purveyor of that quality), her libido is simply not an issue. Honey is free to dress glamorously and flirt about with men of her choosing, but sexually-charged mayhem never ensues. She also understands men and unhesitatingly employs her looks and feminine wiles to lure criminal suspects while scouting out a weakness. To Honey, a baited hook (namely, herself) is simply another tool in her crime-fighting arsenal and she plies it as the situation warrants. Honey is also highly proficient in several forms of martial arts, including karate and judo, and quite adept at defending herself or subduing a suspect. Cool and brassy in the face of danger, this televised manifestation certainly depicts women in a more positive light than the "sexsational private eyeful" of her pulp predecessor.[4]

The series also parts company with the novels by formally pairing her with partner Sam Bolt, apparently a childhood friend who was working for her father when she took over the business. Bolt, vivaciously played by John Ericson, is a handsome hunk in the Bond mold, but also crass, less-than-sagacious on occasion, and somewhat overprotective. Consistent with the job description, he also exudes physicality like Honey, being tall, well-built, and adept at fighting. Bolt clobbers several good-sized opponents throughout the series in some excellently choreographed fight scenes. Overall, their personal relations appear cordial and professional, if mildly flirtatious, as one might expect from two old acquaintances. Sex remains a second banana that never gets peeled. Still, some of their best on-screen chemistry occurs during spats over her rashness and willingness to court danger. On several occasions, Sam lambastes her for lifting evidence from a crime scene, cavalierly exposing herself to harm, and he insists that she "play by the rules" It never occurs to him that Honey, embodying the new, modern women, simply abides by her own.[5]

Rounding out the cast is Irene Hervey as Aunt Meg, who apparently shares the same luxurious hustings as her niece and who functions mainly as comic relief. She also periodically referees Sam and Honey during their many scrapes, perhaps wishing that the two would get married and make their ongoing battle part of marital bliss. Curiously, Meg is no slouch in detective matters and in one episode she conveniently picks the pocket of an intruder who tied her up. But other than serving as a somewhat ditzy firewall between Honey and Sam, she remains a marginal character and in all likelihood would have been written out of the series had it matured into a second season. Another enduring presence on *Honey West,* and among the best remembered, is Bruce the ocelot, a four-legged bit of exotica consistent with spy-type fare of the period. To many, he is an undisguised sexual metaphor–thereby an extension–of Honey herself, being attractive, desirable, affectionate, yet unpredictably snarly and way too dicey to toy with. He is also an interesting counterpoint to Honey's own feline qualities of sensuousness and lethality. An attractive set piece, Bruce had little to do in each episode than bear fangs at newcomers as she ("He" is actually a female) inevitably did to cast members. Nonetheless, pictures of Anne and her garrulous pet are iconic to *Honey West* and the ocelot is fondly remembered by many devotees of the series.

In the Zeitgeist of Bond films and televised spy show like *The Man from U.N.C.L.E.*, *Honey West* is also festooned with its share of high-tech wizardry that the protagonists employed in each episode. This arsenal includes exploding gas earrings, gas-cartridge pens, a garter-belt gas mask worn by Honey, and numerous hidden microphones in pens, lipstick tubes, martini olives, and diamond necklaces. The two even operate miniature radios hidden in their sunglasses while Honey employs another concealed in her jeweled compact. The duo also owned a faux-TV repair truck deceptively labeled "H. W. Bolt & Co. TV Service," which is outfitted with an array of electronic eavesdropping and telephoto equipment. The final toy in Honey's ensemble is her 1965 Shelby Cobra 289 roadster. This essentially is a diminutive British chassis powered by a small-block American V-8 motor (huge by European standards) that has been shoe-horned under the hood, and in which Honey tools around town, looking glamorous in sunglasses as her flaxen mane wafts in the breeze. After all, this was the age of the so-called 'British Invasion," and if Honey could not afford Bond's Aston-Martin, her spiffy, smart-looking Cobra dovetailed nicely with the racy persona she projected. A cool, jazzy theme scored by composer Joseph Mullendore also accentuates the undeniable hip nature of the show and its main character.

The end result is a delectable and unmistakable slice of early 1960s Americana, endearing and enduring in equal measure.

Honey West debuted on September 17, 1965 to basically good reviews while the Nielsen ratings placed it at a respectable tie for 19th place. Still, purists among the critic crowd bemoaned its somewhat meager (low-budget) production values. This was despite the fact that the series routinely utilized overlapping and unmistakably snappy dialogue, innovative camera angles, and clever jump-cuts long before they became industry standards. It also featured innovative casting of such soon-to-be-notable actors as Joe Don Baker, Wayne Rogers, Ray Danton, Richard Kiel, and Michael J. Pollard, some of whom became cult figures in their own right. The overall effect was sexy, campy fun: slick to behold and consciously tongue-in-cheek. But what proved fatal to the series' survival was the Friday night prime-time lineup. *Honey West* found itself pitted against an 800-pound programming gorilla–*Gomer Pyle, U.S.M.C.*–and got clobbered in the ratings. The show was further hurt by weak lead-ins preceding it, prompting many viewers to tune in to NBC or CBS and remain there all evening. Strong talk ensued that the show could revive its fortunes by switching over to color and a one-hour format, but in the end money trumped all other considerations. *Honey West* was basically cancelled because ABC could pay less for the *Avengers* when it debuted on American airwaves in the fall of 1966. So, laurels for the most memorable symbol of modern womanhood went to a leather-clad Diana Rigg, even though *Honey West* enjoys the unimpeachable quality of being first. Its early and unwarranted demise notwithstanding, the show was nominated for an Emmy and received the Mystery Writers of America award for Best Television Series of the Year. Anne Francis was also honored by receipt of a well-deserved Golden Globe Award for her outstanding work. *Honey West* certainly broke the mold as far as televised portrayals of women go and helped upend the prevailing social dogma respecting independent women. Afterwards, strong female leads became desirable

Anne Francis beams after receiving her well-deserved Golden Globe award for Honey West.

broadcast commodities and shows like *The Girl from U.N.C.L.E.*, *Police Woman*, and *Charlie's Angels* proliferated. Still, one scholar bemoans that fifteen years lapsed before the networks dared place a women in charge of her own detective business again.[6]

I conclude this disquisition on an entirely personal note, one perhaps inevitably and inextricably bound up in human nature. When *Honey West* debuted in the fall of 1965, I was but a mere lad of 12 and tabula rasa as far as members of the allegedly weaker sex went. Much to my pre-pubescent amazement, I found myself attracted to Anne Francis in manners that I could neither fathom nor rationalize at the time. You might say that *Honey West* bequeathed to me my first bona fide hormone surge, something that males from this impressionable age recall with relish. In this sense, the series was also a rite of passage for, hereafter, I never quite beheld those mysterious creatures called women in quite the same way. And what a visage Anne presented to young, inquiring minds: a smart, savvy woman, fearless and completely dedicated to her craft. Undoubtedly, many girls of my age were similarly struck by the same *joie de vivre* Anne radiated in the title role, if for entirely different reasons.[7] Compared to the staid female role models preceding her on television, *Honey West* was everything that the emerging social paradigm allowed a woman to be. Hence, my reminiscences about the series are couched in a unique dichotomy. Having shed and evolved beyond the social conventions of my youth, I freely acknowledge Anne Francis for her demonstrated intelligence, varied acting talents, and the impressive longevity of her career. But in *Honey West* she was also an in-your-face, male-wish fantasy and I embrace my inner Neanderthal by forever cherishing those daunting blue eyes, the sexy mole, that sixties flip-do, flipped to perfection, that husky voice, and pantherine form lurking beneath a skin-tight suit. In sum, Anne was the first smokin' hot babe I ever beheld, gloriously female in appearance, speech, and deportment. In fact, her portrayal of *Honey West* remains appealing simply because she never forsook her femininity, even in the rough-and-tumble world of private investigating. Feminists may cringe over so physical an assessment, but I–and perhaps many male viewers of my generation–am forever grateful to Anne for breathing life, and so much more, into television's first female detective. Moreover, the show's enduring popularity transcends mere gender considerations and survives in the minds of many as a true cult series, never to be forgotten. The recent release of Honey West on DVD also assures that a new crop of aficionados will arise in our wake for many, if not all, of the reasons outlined above.[8] Perhaps this is the greatest efficacy that any program can justly aspire.

Gloria Fickling

A NATIVE OF NEW YORK CITY, Gloria (Gautraud) Fickling relocated to Los Angeles, California, and found work as assistant fashion editor of *Look Magazine*. This was followed by a stint at the May Company as their premier stylist, working in concert with noted photographers Hal Adams and John Engstead. Her career received a major boost when she began covering the fashion market for *Women's Daily Wear*, and was also entrusted with designing her own line of maternity wear. More important, Gloria met her future husband, Forrest "Skip" Fickling (1925-1998), a distinguished World War II veteran, while vacationing on Catalina Island and they eloped in Las Vegas on May 21, 1949. The Korean War necessitated the couple moving from Los Angeles to Laguna Beach once Skip was recalled to active duty. Afterwards, he resumed his career at Laguna as a publicity director, while as also dabbling in fiction as a writer. In 1956 Skip contacted his friend, writer Richard Prather, who had created the successful detective character Shell Scott. He broached the idea of a female private eye to him, a novel idea that Prather turned down for want of time and suggested that he do it. Most fortuitously, Skip was up to the challenge and he conceived Honey West as a sexy cross between Marilyn Monroe and Mike Hammer. With Gloria acting as editor and consultant, he went on to write *This Girl for Hire* in only 25 days under the pseudonym "G. G. (Gloria Gautraud) Fickling."

A month-long trip to New York City to haunt publishing houses ensued, but the novel was finally picked by Pyramid Books and sold 250,000 copies in its first printing. Between 1957 and 1971 Skip and Gloria collaborated on no less than eleven *Honey West* novels, which sold 7 million copies worldwide. In 1965 the series was also picked up as a program for ABC, which further spawned a *Honey West* action figure, a *Honey West* game, and a *Honey West* comic book. The Ficklings also briefly operated a "Honey West"-themed nightclub in Laguna Beach for several months.

After Skip died of a brain tumor on April 3, 1998, Gloria remained active as a restaurant reporter with the *Orange County Register*. One of the best-known and most beloved residents of Laguna Beach, she continues working for local charities such as the community clinic, the Resource and Relief Center, and Rescuing Unwanted Furry Friends (RUFF). She remains a standard fixture at arts and fashion events throughout the county, invariably decked-out in one of her trademark, outlandish hats.

JF: Gloria, I want you to briefly describe your life before you met Skip. Where are you from and what did you do?

Gloria: Well, I was really in the fashion industry when I met Skip. I was writing for *Women's Wear Daily*. I was an assistant fashion editor at *Look Magazine* first. Boy, that really dates me–I am still 29 though, I want to make that *very* clear to everyone! So I went from *Look Magazine* to work at the May Company in the fashion department, I was the coordinator. At that time the May Company was doing all their newspaper advertising with photographs, all the other departments did sketches, artwork. So I worked with a fabulous photographer, Al Adams, so I was in everyday putting up work for newspaper advertising, which was really exciting.

JF: What time frame?

Gloria: We're talking like 1948-1949. That's when I was with *Women's Wear Daily* – I got hired from one job to another, I never really looked for a job. And I was on Catalina Island with my sister and aunt and a cousin, and we were girls over there having a good time celebrating my sister's birthday. I was getting dressed in my rainbow-striped two-piece bathing suit and I got locked in the beach house room. I couldn't get out! The only alternative was lift the window and crawl out backwards! And Skip is sitting there watching every move. And later he said, "I thought you were some kind of second-story girl." As we went along, I think I would do certain things that germinated in Skip's mind the Honey West character. She had a lot of my characteristics. And that's how I met him.

JF: Was it you or Skip that came up with Honey West in the fifties?

Gloria: It was Slip that came up with Honey West, but everyone though I wrote the books because there was so much of my persona in the character.

JF: Are you really that reckless?

Gloria: Not quite. We had to embellish it somehow [laughter]. But after I met him that day, here's another little Honey West twist you'll see. We got talking and I said I'm out and about and he said, "Would you meet me later, maybe we'll get together for a hamburger or something." "Okay, fine. I'm going to a party earlier, but I'll meet you later on." So I went to the party–Honey West again–this guy tried to nail me on a table and I took my two feet, and remember, I'm five feet tall, 98 pounds, and I knocked him across the room and ran like Hell. By the time I got back to the inn where we were staying, there was Skip. A little groggy from having drank a lot of beer waiting for me, and so that kind of started it. And he went to church with me on Catalina the next day, and then changed his route back to get on the same boat I was on–and we danced all the way back. And we danced ever since. Good-looking guy, smart, close to my age, the first time I'd ever met a guy that I could carry on an intelligent conversation when you're like 19 and 20. Guys at that age were just into fun and games. But he was brilliant. You could have a conversation with him and he was interested in people. It wasn't love at first sight–it was provocative.

JF: What was the reaction to the first *Honey West* novel–a big success?

Gloria: Yes! It was 1956, I think. I am not good at remembering dates. Skip was a crackerjack at that.

JF: So success basically bred success. You did eleven novels.

Gloria: Eleven. And I think the way we sold it is a remarkable story because we couldn't get an agent, and I was so convinced that Skip had a great idea so I said, "You know what, we'll just farm the kids out to my parents and we'll fly out to New York. And, boy, we didn't have much money, so we said we can afford 30 days in New York because I had relatives there we could stay with, so that helped. But on the 30th day we sold the book to these two wonderful Jewish men at Pyramid Books, Mat Hutner, a tall handsome man, and his partner Al Plane, a guy with one arm. And Al was the one who just fell in love with us. He loved the book, he loved everything about it. We'd have a meeting and he'd say, "Come back at five o'clock, we'll have a cocktail." Then he'd unlock his little box and pour the drinks and we'd spend like an hour just talking. That was great. Another interesting facet is that the editor at Pyramid, a woman, didn't like the idea, and I said, Well, the publishers like it so we're going to go for it." "Well, you'd better change that name, 'Honey West,' it's *never* going to sell." Hello? "Well guess what, we are not going to change the name." And how Skip came up with the name was we were living on High Drive here in Laguna at the time and he would sit out on the back patio and type his manuscripts and asked, "What does every guy call the woman he loves? Honey. And here we are in the west so we'll call her 'Honey West.'" That was it and we never changed it.

JF: So how many *Honey West* novels were sold, all told?

Gloria: I know that at one point we had 10 million in world sales. Another thing I was told, but I never tried to look it up, was *Encyclopedia Britannica* saying that Honey West was the most famous female fictional character in the world.

JF: So when did you make the transition from novels to television?

Gloria: Skip was very determined that we were going to do that and William Morris was our agent at the time and he kept pushing on it and pushing on it.

JF: How did it end up in the lap of Aaron Spelling?

Gloria: I don't think I have an answer for that, but he was the one who showed an interest in it and things moved quickly. Skip and I were in Newport Beach one night having a drink at the bar in a trendy restaurant and the two guys sitting next to us were saying, "How about that, Honey West is going to be a television show." What?! So we started talking to them and they had the information and that's how we found out.

JF: You were the last ones to know! Did you get to meet Aaron Spelling at any point?

Gloria: Oh, yes. A little scrawny runt of a guy with a really great ego. But he knew how to make money. I think to this day they say that his mansion is the most expensive ever.

JF: So *Honey West* is in production in 1965. Were you on top of the world?

Gloria: Oh, we were! Absolutely, that's when we built the penthouse. Up until about a year ago, when I had the new patio done, we had a slab there that said, "The House that Honey West Built." There's a little chunk of it we were able to save that's in the driveway. And it was the TV series that got us this, but we got kinda of a raw deal.

JF: How so?

Gloria: William Morris said, "Send us a contract saying we are no longer your agents, we are your friend" – they took 90 percent and gave up 10 percent. You learn the hard way. But when it came to getting all the fine print and everything together, Skip said, "I think we should get a full screen credit." Okay, William Morris took advantage, but at least we should get a full screen credit. Aaron Spelling said no to the full screen credit. "What do you mean? Why not a full screen credit?" So one of his henchmen took us out to lunch and said, "Now, come on, you've got to do this. You know, it's gone too far now. You can't break the contract." Well, they [finally] went along with it and so, in retribution, Aaron Spelling said, "We won't buy any scripts from the Ficklings." So they never used our scripts and we had dynamite ideas.

JF: Were you ever on the production set of *Honey West*?

Gloria: Oh, yes, a couple of times.

JF: What did you think of Anne Francis? Did you like her as the choice?

Gloria: We *loved* her as the choice! We just thought we couldn't ask for anyone better.

JF: Did you get to meet her personally?

Gloria: Yes, but she was very cool, the antithesis of John Ericson, who was a real sweetheart and we invited him up to the house. Anne was very standoffish. I have a feeling that it was a Spelling thing against us. We always thought that, anyway. So we have to say "allegedly."

JF: But you did like John Ericson?

Gloria: We loved John. Please tell him I would love to hear from him. We really enjoyed his friendship.

JF: So *Honey West* came and went, it lasted one season and the network decided to cancel it because they could get the *Avengers* for less money.

Gloria: It was on the books, it was a last-minute decision. It was all set to go; we were going to be in color–all of a sudden gone. Talk about a kick in the butt, was that a letdown.

JF: And since that day you've not receive any money or residuals from the show? *Honey West* has been on TV several times since then.

Gloria: I think TV Land did a whole day of *Honey West*, a marathon!

JF: Do you get a lot of mail about *Honey West* over the years from people of my generation?

Gloria: Not that much, occasionally, but I walk down the street, even if I am out of town, a car will come up and go "Honey West." I am very well known in town.

JF: So what are your plans for the future? What would you like to see done with *Honey West*?

Gloria: I would desperately want to see that movie made. That was the wrap up; books, the TV, and a major movie. I sold the franchise rights, that was a thing, too.

JF: So you basically watched your show go on the air, knowing that it's beyond your reach. You've not received the credit or money for your own show.

Gloria: I think we can't trust anybody anymore. Before we sold the TV rights, people were coming up to us right and left. And we almost got ripped off early from people coming in from nowhere that wanted us to sign contracts. *Honey West* was very hot long before the TV rights. A lot of people saw the potential. It was quite amazing.

JF: You know what? I hope they do not make the movie because they'll only mess it up. They'll kill it like they kill everything else. Reese Witherspoon is *not* a Honey West type.

Gloria: I didn't think so earlier when they talked about her, but she's really matured beautifully.

JF: But she's such an elegant Southern belle I just cannot picture her kicking guys in the teeth. I just can't see it [laughter].

Gloria: She is one helluva an actress, though.

JF: She is but, as a matter of fact, if I were to bring *Honey West* back as a TV show, my first problem is where am I going to find a woman with the beauty and talent of Anne Francis? I don't think that can be done today. Looking back over the years, do you consider *Honey West* one of the high points of your life?

Gloria: Absolutely! People have been begging me to write my story, I've had such a fascinating life, and I stated it a year ago and worked on it for a couple of months, then I decided to put it aside. I am busy with a lot of other stuff. I've done restaurant reviews since the mid-'60s—I've migrated from fashion to food!

Bibliography

McClellan, Dennis. "Honey's Back in Town: The Book is Not Yet Closed on the 'Sexiest Private Eye' to Grace a Cover." *Los Angeles Times* December 17, 1986, D1.

Smith, Kevin B. "Eyewitness Double Trouble: *Honey West* and Her Stylish Creator Gloria Fickling." *Mystery Scene* No. 86 (Fall 2004): 46-48.

Takahama, Valerie. "True 'West': Gloria Fickling helped Create Honey West. Now the Fictional P.I. is Making a Comeback." *Orange County Register* November 9, 2005, 1.

Contact

Gloria Fickling
490 Hilledge Drive
Laguna Beach, CA 92651-1917

Anne Francis

ANNE LLOYD FRANCIS was born in Ossining, New York, on September 16, 1930, and at the age of five she began modeling with the Robert Powers Agency to assist her family during the Great Depression. A beautiful child with a distinct mole to the right of her lower lip, she was also featured on the cover of *Ladies' Home Journal*. Anne made her Broadway debut at the age of eleven, and also appeared in some of the earliest television broadcasts before that medium was sidelined by World War II. She first ventured to Hollywood in 1946 and won a small role in the film *Summer Holiday* (1948) starring Mickey Rooney. When nothing further materialized, she returned to New York and made regular appearances on live TV. In 1950 she appeared as a youthful prostitute in *So Young, So Bad* for United Artists with two other future notables, Anne Jackson and Rita Moreno. The five-foot, eight-inch tall Anne came to the attention of 20th Century-Fox, which signed her for *Elopement* (1951), opposite William Lundigan, and she also appeared in her first big-budget effort, *Lydia Bailey* (1952), the following year. She was touted by the studio as "The Palomino Blonde," and two years later became an MGM contract player. At MGM, Anne appeared with Spencer Tracy, Robert Ryan and John Ericson in *Bad Day at Black Rock* (1954), as the sympathetic wife of Glenn Ford in the cult favorite *Blackboard Jungle* (1955) and the science-fiction classic *Forbidden Planet* (1956), in which she pioneered mini-skirts long before they became popular. Her final picture for MGM was *Don't Go Near the Water* (1957), at which point she was released from her contract and worked freelance. Her most memorable work in this regard was the independently-produced *Girl of the Night* (1960, in which she played a prostitute undergoing psychotherapy.

Anne spent the first half of the 1960s on television and filmed like *Satan Bug* and *Brainstorm* (both 1965) before landing the leading character in *Honey West*. This is arguably the role for which she is justly celebrated, given restrictions on female casting from those days. In an age of James Bond and beautiful accomplices, Anne simply stood out and also had the talent to make *Honey West's* private investigator a believable, likeable character that transcended the show's technical shortcomings (30 minutes, black and white). This is all the more impressive considering that Anne, then thirty-five, was at an age when most Hollywood actresses were routinely put out to pasture. A meticulous perfectionist, Anne studied Okinawa Te karate under Sensei Gordon Doversola for two hours a day and insisted in doing many of her own stunts. *Honey West* remains a cult favorite among TV viewers of that generation, despite its early cancellation. Anne continued with movies for the rest of the decade but by the 1970s had shifted more or less over to guest spots on television. She went into semi-retirement in 2004 and can look back upon an incredible oeuvre of work stretching back nearly seven decades! A survivor of two rough divorces, psychotherapy sessions, and cancer surgery, Anne continues enjoying life to the fullest in Santa Barbara, California.

JF: Anne, I want you to briefly describe your career before you encountered Aaron Spelling.

Anne: I started when I was five, modeling, and then I started in radio when I was seven with children's broadcasting on NBC and CBS. And then when I was 10, I did a daily TV program with an actress who played my mother, and the two of us would read children's books while an artist named Johnny Roupe would draw pictures. In December of 1941 all television was stopped and frozen until after the war and I continued with doing radio broadcasting. Then I went for one year to MGM, when I was 13, and did two days' work on a film called *Summer Holiday* with Mickey Rooney, Walter Huston, Agnes Moorehead, and Marilyn Maxwell – really, really fun people, and that all happened kind of strangely. Then I went back to New York and back to modeling and then I did a film called *So Young, So Bad*. I just happened to have taken some pictures up to this particular production company a week or two before because a gal friend suggested it-we all used to help each other-and then somebody else a week later said, "You ought to go up to such-and-such and take some pictures," you know, and meet the casting director. So I went and because I went up in the elevator I thought, "This is very familiar"–and as I walked out the elevator door I realized I'd been there the week before. So I said, "This is silly, you already saw me last week," and at that moment the director of the film peered around the corner and said, "Come in here," so I went in and they had me read the part of a girl who was a prostitute. This is all about girls in a reform school-and that's how I got that part. It's been weird all along the way with these strange kinds of coincidences that have taken place, and bringing it up to Aaron Spelling.

JF: What was your first impression of Aaron Spelling?

Anne: Well, I didn't have any first impression since he walked by the table where my agent and I were sitting in the old Brown Derby, and he just sort of waved and said hello to my agent. I really didn't know him. And my agent chatted with me some and was talking to me about a series and such and I said, "I don't want to go near a series." I saw what happened to all these different friends, it's grueling work and it just looks like it's awful. He said, "Well, just supposing you had your choice of the kind of series you'd like to do." And I said, "Oh, probably something adventurous, something fun, and something kind of detective-ish like a female Amos Burke." Anyway, we went on talking about it and the next day Bill called me and said, "Are you and Aaron Spelling playing a game with me?" And I said, "What do you mean, I don't even know him!" Well, he said, "I just got a call from him saying that he's working on a new series that going to be a spin off from *Burke's Law* and he thinks you'd be perfect for the partner–a gal named Honey West." I went up to the office, met with him, and read the script—and that's how that happened. All these things have happened in very odd ways.

JF: What is your impression as John Ericson as an actor?

Anne: Well, John I knew already because we had worked together in *Bad Day at Black Rock*, he was my brother. So I was delighted that John got it.

JF: Describe a typical day on the set of *Honey West*. Was it really hectic?

Anne: Yes, it was long hours, Twelve-hour days–sometimes toward the end of the week they'd climb up to seventeen, eighteen hours. Normally, during the week when you shot, the union rule was when you finished at seven o'clock at night they could not call you in until seven the following morning. If on a Friday you finished at nine o'clock at night, they could call you in at seven. It was long and it was hard, but it was a lot of fun. We had a *great* crew–they were all guys and all the happy-go-lucky kind. We really had a terrific time working together there.

JF: Did you really get into the character of Honey West, because everybody says you made it look so easy.

Anne: Oh, I don't know why. I was just enjoying myself!

JF: So, you never had a real affinity for Honey West? It was just another job for you?

Anne: No, it wasn't just another job. I wouldn't have taken a series if I thought it was just another job! Not with those hours. No, it was different, it was fun. I hadn't seen any other shows with a gal who was able to do all of these things. I worked with Gordon Doversola, as you know, for a couple of weeks ahead of time before we started. And that bit of training helped me tremendously a few years later when I was in the theater. It was a Saturday night, we had finished a play, and all the others were opting to go out to dinner and I said, "You know, I don't think I feel like it, I feel like just going home." So I said goodnight to them and, of course, all the crowds from the audience had disappeared, so I started on down the stairs into the bowels of the Ahmanson Theater, and as I finished the first flight [of stairs] I thought I heard footsteps behind me. Then the second flight, they were coming closer. On the third flight there was no question, there was somebody coming down those stairs. The place was empty, the crowd had all dispersed, and I came to the realization that "I'd better do something!" before I got to the bottom of that flight of stairs. And from the karate that I had learned, I realized that since I was on the stairs below, whoever was behind me, I had the advantage. And so I just whirled around, grabbed the banister with one hand and I was ready for whatever moves this person made. By this point he was about three steps behind me–and we just locked eyes, stared at each other. And then he finally said, "Did I startle you?" and I said "No." So we both froze for like two or three seconds, probably, but it felt like forever for me. He finally turned around and went back up the stairs–and I ran down the stairs and then got into my car and then I fell apart–slammed the door and said, "Oh, my God!" [laughter]

JF: Well, for a few seconds there you *were* Honey West.

Anne: I *was* Honey West! [laughter] And I had not been Honey West for some time but I remembered that move. I knew that if he made a move toward me, he would go down the stairs, over me. I knew that I might get hurt, but so would he.

JF: Well, describe Gordon as an instructor. Was he friendly and outgoing, or was he stern?

Anne: Gordon? Oh, no, he was very warm, very friendly, very much so.

JF: He has a picture of you training on the beach–did you train at the beach a lot?

Anne: No, most of it was on the back lot.

JF: Did you enjoy karate?

Anne: Yes, I did! I haven't pursued it since I did the show, but I enjoyed it when I was doing it.

JF: Describe Sharon Lucas to me.

Anne: Sharon still had her Oklahoma accent and she was really very down to earth. She had an invincible quality about her, which is why it was sad the way she was hurt. She was in *How the West was Won*, she was supposed to catapult out of a building with this young man, and he was new to the business. He just did not fall right and she ended up with a broken neck. And that kind of finished her career. She was really so helpful to people, generous, and just a lovely lady. I was most fond of her.

JF: You were at Gene LeBell's roast about three or four years ago–what did you say about him?

Anne: I think I said something to the effect that there was only one woman I knew who could take him on–and that would be Sharon Lucas. He got red–I think that they had dated some, so …

JF: Do you remember Irene Hervey at all?

Anne: Irene Hervey? She was charming. She was cute. Just fun.

JF: What was your relationship to John Ericson? Was he just a big friend to you?

Anne: We talked about the characters ahead of time and one of the main things that I felt was important was that if this show succeeds there would probably be a lot of young people and kids watching it. So I said, "Johnny, let's stay away from the booze and the cigarettes on the screen." And we did. We made a pact with each other that we were not going to smoke on screen, we weren't going to drink.

JF: A lot of people remember Bruce the Ocelot, what was he like?

Anne: Ocelots don't like hot lights, so he was pretty consistent.

He didn't enjoy himself acting. Picking him up would be like picking up a bunch of snakes–two feet would be going in one direction and two feet would be going in the other. I used to have to get a tetanus shot every two weeks. And he wasn't mean, he just didn't enjoy ... you know, he was not a born actor.

JF: Did you like driving that little white car?

Anne: You mean the little Cobra? Oh, yeah, that was fun! It was a hot little car and, boy, you could stop on a dime. And you could brake it right up to the edge of a cliff and stop.

JF: Did you consider *Honey West* to be "cutting edge" as far as women's portrayals on the screen were concerned?

Anne: I don't think so; I don't think I thought that much about it. I just thought it was a fun series, a show that had not been done before.

JF: What was your relationship to Aaron Spelling after *Honey West*?

Anne: I did a few *Fantasy Islands* for him, but I didn't really see much of him after that.

JF: Looking back over a long and distinguished career, how do you evaluate *Honey West*? As just another show?

Anne: No, not from the letters that I get. I still get letters from people who grew up–kind of–with Honey, and the women who felt that she gave them courage to break the model of what women were in the '60s. Also, I've gotten letters from men who kinda fell for Honey, but also liked the fact that she was bright and capable and could stand alongside a man, so I thought that was kind of interesting. A little bit of education went on there and we didn't even realize it.

JF: Well, I was twelve years old when *Honey West* came out. You know, that impressionable age—and you were my first girlfriend!

Anne: Awwwww…

JF: Let me ask you this: What would convince you to go back to acting? If you got a good script or a good role? You still do not consider yourself retired yet.

Anne: Mostly [retired], but not completely. I mean, if I fell in love with it. Yep, it would fun!

Bibliography

Francis, Anne. *Voices from Home: An Inner Journey*. Milbrae, Calif.: Celestial Arts, 1982.

Listanti, Tom, and Louis Paul. *Film Fatales: Women in Espionage Films and Television, 1962-1963*. Jefferson, N.C.: McFarland, 2002.

Parish, James R., and Ronald L. Bowers. *The MGM Stock Company*. New Rochelle, N.Y.: Arlington House Publishers, 1973.

Smith, Ronald L. Smith. *Sweethearts of 60's TV*. New York: S.P.I Books, 1993.

Wagner, Laura. "Anne Francis: Down to Earth" *Films of the Golden Age* No. 55 (Winter 2008): 50-73.

Contact

Anne Francis
PO Box 5608
Santa Barbara, CA 91350-5608
www.AnneFrancis.net

John Ericson

BORN JOSEPH MEIBES in Düsseldorf, Germany, on September 25, 1927, John migrated to the United States with his family in the 1930s and lived in Chicago, Illinois, and Detroit, Michigan, before settling down in Elmhurst, New York. His father worked for the food-flavoring industry while his mother was a former Shakespearean actress and operatic singer. John studied acting at the American Academy of Dramatic Arts in New York City (Marlon Brando and Don Rickles were two of his classmates) and worked with several summer stock companies until 1949. That year he was tapped by director Fred Zinnemann to star in the MGM motion picture, *Teresa* (1951), opposite Pier Angeli. Soon afterwards, John landed a noted part on Broadway in the original stage production of *Stalag 17* and, after production ceased in 1952, he began filling slots in radio and television programs. Another big break came by playing movie roles with Elizabeth Taylor in *Rhapsody* (1954), Edmund Purdom in *The Student Prince* (1954), and Grace Kelly in *Green Fire* (1954). In 1955 he performed his most important work at MGM by appearing in the seminal production *Bad Day at Black Rock* (1955), starring Spencer Tracy, Robert Ryan, and Anne Francis. In all these MGM pictures, John was cast as somebody else's brother and garnered little critical attention for his smooth and urbane style of acting. He left MGM's stable the following year and began appearing in numerous B pictures for the rest of the decade. Foremost among these was starring as the title role in *Pretty Boy Floyd* (1960).

John returned to television in the early 1960s, with little fanfare, until 1965, when he was reunited with Anne Francis on *Honey West*. Here, he played Honey's macho and cantankerous partner Sam Bolt with aplomb-and greatly relieved that, for once, he was not cast as somebody's younger brother! The show was cancelled after a single season, and then John became a standard fixture in Hollywood and European B pictures for the remainder of his career. Foremost among his credits was the Disney production of *Bedknobs and Broomsticks* (1971), in which he played a Nazi officer defeated by enchanted armor, and *The Bamboo Saucer* (1969), a Cold War science-fiction thriller. Since retiring from the business, John settled down in Santa Fe, New Mexico, where he remains active in local theater activities and landscape painting.

JF: You were working on the set of *Bad Day at Black Rock* and you were introduced to an actress named Anne Francis, who is also from New York. What did you think of her? What was your first impression?

John: Oh, she was terrific. She got along really great with men and she became like one of the boys and she would hold court. And when the guys chummed together, she'd be part of that-she was a great deal of fun. I liked her a lot and she was the only female in that story. And I remember Spencer Tracy, whom I liked so much-it was a great cast. I was so lucky to be in that and, by the way, Dory Schary wanted me for this part. He had given me the script when I was there under contract at Metro and they wanted me to do this. Finally, Dory started calling my house, saying, "John, I really want you to do this!" I called him back and I said, "Okay, Dory, I will do your script because it's a wonderful story, but I want to make sure I don't do just brothers all the time–nice guys all the time.

JF: Moving right ahead, into television: What did you think of Aaron Spelling?

John: Oh, I thought he was one helluva nice guy. And he used to come on the set all the time; in those days it was very homey and we were all like a family, you know what I mean? It's not much like that anymore.

JF: Was *Burke's Law* the first time you were reunited with Anne Francis?

John: Yeah, that's the first time. At that time there were two leading men–one was the lawyer type and then there was the roughneck-type ex-Marine who was her partner who always got her out of a jam. And I thought, "Oh, that's interesting. I like that!" So I went in to read for it and Aaron Spelling liked me and so they signed me. And I made a great friend in Don Engles, who did a lot of scripts, and he's still around and he's still writing.

JF: So what did you think of your character, Sam Bolt, the rugged ex-Marine?

John: Oh, I just loved that part. That's what I was ready for as an actor. He's got humor, he's got pizzazz, he's got guts. He gets along great. And he had action scenes and I loved action, I loved the stuff Burt Lancaster was doing–all that action stuff, I loved that. Body movement and all that. And when they did the pilot they said, "Okay, we want you and Anne, but we're not going to use the lawyer part." And I thought, Boy, that's great, more for me to do. And so that how I got it and I did it.

JF: So do you consider Sam Bolt one of the high points of your career?

John: Yes, yes, yes! That was a very interesting part and I was very relaxed in doing it. And I always mentioned, when people talked about it, that it was like a boy/girl James Bond. And it was, because we had all those little gimmicks and all the fighting and rescuing, and it was very innovative.

JF: Well, Anne took karate lessons to do the Honey West role. Did they give you boxing lessons or any fighting techniques?

John: Yeah, I was getting to be very natural at it. I didn't need many lessons because I was athletic as a kid. And I was always very impressed with body movements like yoga, ballet, and stuff, although I never took ballet but I loved it because I loved what they did with their bodies. And I loved the way Burt Lancaster used his body in his expressions. I really liked all that, not just the words, use your whole body to do the acting, and your mind and your soul inside. And that's what it's all about.

JF: So you had fun doing *Honey West*?

John: Oh, you know what I did one time? That episode "Slay, Gypsy, Slay," [where] I was the old man when I came to rescue her. I put on the makeup and everything and I decided to go over to the *Smothers Brothers* set in that costume–that whole get-up that I had on—while waiting for our next shot. They were shooting on the same lot and I walked in and went [*old man's voice*] "Heah! Heah! Heah!" and they were just flabbergasted going, "Who the hell *is* this guy?" They didn't recognize me–I had so much fun doing that. And I thought, "Boy, this is great. This series is going to allow me to do different things now, things that I'm not used to." But then it ended that year. We were going to come back and do the series as an hour show and I thought, "Fantastic!"... and two days later they called and said it was cancelled, Aaron said ABC doesn't like the show. They took our budget away from us and the last few episodes were far less elegant because we couldn't go on location anymore, we didn't have the money. ABC just didn't want that show.

JF: What was your relationship with Anne at this time? You both professionals, but were you also friends? She tells me that you both spent long, grueling hours on the set, sometimes up to 18 hours at a time. How did you work and not get at each other's throats?

John: Well, we didn't. She kept along very well and it never bothered me that she was always the center of attention. She used to go out with some of the crew people and eat in the restaurant afterwards, have a few drinks and laugh. And I would more or less listen–I wouldn't do a lot. And the crew used to say, "God, John, doesn't it bother you that she's so macho?" You know, the center of attention. And I said, "No, I'm not worried about my manhood. I enjoy her, she's great." And when she would hold court and tell stories and everything, she'd look over at me and go, "Isn't that right, John?" And I'd go, "That's absolutely right!" I'd agree with her. It was really a great, great relationship.

JF: Well, those fight scenes in *Honey West* look really intense. It looked like you guys were really trading punches!

John: Oh, yeah! They were good—*they were fun*! Another part of using your whole body to express a scene. And it was great–I loved that. As I said, that's why I liked Burt Lancaster, because he was a trapeze artist.

JF: Well, do you consider *Honey West* one of the highlights of your career?

John: Yes, I do. Absolutely. It was the only series I ever did and, frankly, I am surprised I did not do any other series.

JF: Do you get a lot of inquiries about *Honey West*? Are people contacting you?

John: Yes, it's great. But I do not want to get involved in fan letters and all that stuff. When I am working, yes, not when I am semi-retired.

JF: So you're still active, then?

John: Oh, yeah, I've done stage plays here in New Mexico. Sometimes they say, "Sorry, we're going to hire someone with experience in Hollywood for the part."

JF: Without realizing you have fifty years of experience behind you! That's sad.

John: I know, yeah. Then they say, "But you look too old now." They don't realize that I still get compliments for looking really good for my age. And I don't have a pot belly; I'm still lean, like I was in *Honey West*.

JF: One last question: Looking back over a long and distinguished career, do you have any regrets? Any leading roles that you just didn't get?

John: I wanted to do the part Jimmy Stewart did for *The Spirit of St. Louis*, because I was more of Lindbergh's age. Yeah, that was really something I wanted to do. The only other thing is that I did not take things into my own hands and push at it, I trusted my agents. It was a big mistake. So I have to say that I am the reason why it didn't happen. I don't blame anybody but me. I didn't get aggressive enough, I was having too much fun just working.

JF: Would you say that they're going to plow you under anyway if they can't make money off you?

John: Yeah, they do.

JF: So when you left that place you had no real regrets, you were probably relieved?

John: I'll tell you, when I left there I became a changed man. Because of the smog in the air there I had developed a yellow pallor to my skin and I had terrible sinus conditions and I'd get these headaches and everything. The smog–it bothered the hell out of me. And I had a friend call me and say, "Before you move, please come to New Mexico"– and I hate the desert — you know, like Palm Springs. And she said, "This is not Palm Springs, it's a high desert, quite different! We have trees, we have mountains, we have springs, we have lakes." And I said, "Okay, okay, we'll come and visit. And when we got there it felt like, suddenly, a veil of peace fell over me. We stood outside in her yard at night looking at beautiful stars. I hadn't seen stars for ten years in Los Angeles because of the smog! It's very quiet and I'm looking at the stars and I started hearing "thump-thump"–and I thought, "What the hell is that?" It was my heartbeat I was hearing! Such silence, it's so amazing.

Bibliography

McMullan, Jim, and Dick Gautier. *Actors as Artists*. Boston: Tuttle, 1992, 44-45.

Minton, Kevin L. "John Ericson." *Classic Images* No. 238 (April 1995): 18, 20, 24.

Nott, Robert. "John Ericson." *Filmfax* No. 66 (April-May, 1998): 103-105+

Parish, Robert, and Ronald L. Bowers. *The MGM Stock Company*. New Rochelle, N.Y.: Arlington House Publishers, 1973.

Contact

John Ericson
7 Avenue Vista Grande #10
Santa Fe, NM 87508-9198

Gene LeBell

GENE LEBELL ENJOYS a long and storied career in both martial arts and motion pictures. Born in Los Angeles, California, on October 9, 1932, he was exposed to competitive sports at an early age and became an exponent of grappling. Relatively short and banty at 165 pounds, he quickly gained notoriety for routinely besting opponents much larger than himself. This expertise came in handy when Gene commenced studying judo, at which he also excelled. He had 14 years of intense training from some of the leading authorities in the world when, to no surprise, he handily won the National Judo Championship in 1954. Critics railed against this red-headed and somewhat brusque interloper flourishing in the then-closed world of martial arts so Gene, in character, proved them all wrong by winning the championship again in 1955. He subsequently parleyed his talents into professional wrestling, triumphing in more than 200 bouts over the next 25 years. Possibly his most famous encounter was against accomplished middleweight boxer Milo Savage in Salt Lake City, Utah, on December 2, 1963, whom Gene disposed of in only four rounds. Concurrently with wrestling, Gene also served as a martial arts instructor and tutored several Hollywood notables and martial arts celebrities such as Chuck Norris, Bruce Lee, Ed Parker, and Bill "Superfoot" Wallace. He remains active in martial arts, still runs his own dojo, and is touted as one of the greatest fighters in contact sports. In recognition of his many feats, he received a 9th Degree Black Belt by the United States Ju-Jitsu Federation in 2000 and a 9th Dan in Kodokan Judo in 2005. Gene remains in demand as a boxing/martial arts referee and has, in the past, overseen ringside clashes of such leading personalities such as Muhammad Ali. He is universally celebrated in sports' circles as "The Godfather of Grappling."

In additional to all the above, Gene has also distinguished himself as one of Hollywood's leading stunt men and stunt trainers to stars like George Reeves in the *Adventures of Superman* TV series. He is a veteran performer of no less that 246 films and television shows. In *Honey West*, he instructed both Sharon Lucas and Anne Francis in many of their karate/judo moves, both of whom became quite adept. In certain scenes he would also appear in drag to execute a judo throw on an adversary too big for Sharon or Anne to handle, where the invariable long shot paraded those sexy legs of his. Moreover, Gene's celebrated grumpiness and rumpled appearance completely masks the fact that he is a gentleman and all-around neat guy. The present writer delights in having survived a sparring session (strictly verbal!) with Gene at his house in June 2008.

JF: Explain briefly how you got into wrestling and martial arts.

Gene: Well, there's no brief in getting into it. My family had an auditorium called the Olympic Auditorium. My mother, Eileen Eaton, was the promoter there for 38 years. She also promoted it for a lot of movies; *Raging Bull*, and the first *Rocky*, a lot of it was shot there. Hundreds of other movies. So to get rid of me when I was seven years old she took me to the LA Athletic Club in Los Angeles where people train for the Olympics in swimming, boxing, wrestling. I was working out with the old pros. The old pros were not clowns, they could really wrestle and the difference between pro-wrestling and amateur is that pro-wrestlers do arm-locks, leg-locks, chokes, whatever. The amateur is Greco-Roman, is only from the waist up, can't grab a leg. Freestyle is waist-up, waist down. Judo has a uniform with a jacket and pants and a belt. Sambo has a jacket only and a belt, and pants that are a little short–I wouldn't want you to think that they go around naked in Sambo. And all the arts usually have their own uniform, the karate usually has the karate gi which is a uniform that is thinner and lighter than the judo suit because you're not grabbing it, you're just throwing punches.

JF: When did you earn the title of the "World's Toughest Man?" How did you go about that?

Gene: I wrestled, I boxed, and since I was mentally sick I used to take on everybody that I thought was tough and see if I could beat him. I won nationals in judo a couple times and was in international competition and all that stuff. All those first-class trophies you see there–you put all those trophies together they don't make one house payment. Now, as a stuntman, I've had every star in Hollywood from John Wayne to Jack Benny to Jim Garner–they've all beat me up.

JF: Okay, now let's back up a minute. How did you get involved in the stunt business?

Gene: When I got into pro-wrestling in 1955 a fellow named Dick Lane called me "Judo Gene LeBell" and I used to take challengers out of the audience or anybody that came into town. We'd check him out, take him down to the gym and see if I could lay some hurt on him, because when you're a sadistic bastard like me–that's sex!

That and racing motorcycles. That's over the handlebars and I don't mean that as an obscene statement. Anyway, I am sure that there's a lot of tough guys there and in *Black Belt Magazine* they named the top twenty toughest guys in the world and they put me at number two. Well, there's a couple of guys that are really good at three, four, and five–and the guy they put at number one I thought couldn't tie his shoes, he was a bartender. I don't care how tough you are in the street; you've got to spend your time in a gym.

JF: So you entered professional sports, you won awards, and became known as an athlete. At what point did you decide to take your skill into stunts?

Gene: Well, when I started pro-wrestling, they needed something with a guy taking a fall. The reason I fall so good is that my mother, who was a Canadian, had a good left hook and she used to knock me down twice a week–sometimes twice on Sunday–because she was very religious. I never did like my mother because in 1963 she cut my allowance off. I loved her but she was a Canadian and I really don't like Canadians. My wife is a Canadian also, but that's a different story. [Laughter]

JF: So when did your career progress to stunt work?

Gene: I got into stunts about 1955. I just started, I worked one day, then I worked a second day, then they kept on calling me in. And, since I rode horses, I got to play Indians. I look like a milk bottle, I am so white, but I have brown eyes so they put a wig on you, a little make-up and get you up at four o'clock in the morning so that you could be an Indian. And then at noon, when it gets to be 110 degrees, you put on one of those wool outfits and you're a Confederate soldier chasing yourself. Never did catch myself. Since then I've been doing stunts ever since. The thing is, in 1960 you began getting residuals, so you work once and then you get residuals when it comes on again and again, and again. I make six figures every year in residuals, which is good. It helps my bad habit, which is eating, but it's been a great life. I've been in Mecca and played with the Gods, I've done every stunt from high vaults to fire, horses, motorcycles, car turnovers. I do a little bit of quick-draw, and little bit of whips and knives, but there are stunt men that are really aces up, they're really good, so they're friends of mine and I push them on things that I don't do that well. But 90 percent of the stuff I do, and that's that.

JF: How did you get involved with the show *Honey West*? Were you approached by Aaron Spelling or was he too high and mighty to contact you?

Gene: You know, since I've been brain-dead, if a guy's high and mighty, if he puts his pants on one leg at a time, I don't know and don't care. They said they wanted me to do a pilot. The gal that doubles Anne was a gal named Sharon Lucas; I could go on for years on her, but I am not going to.

JF: We'll get to Sharon afterwards.

Gene: You don't have to, I never liked her anyway. I think she was a Canadian.

JF: [Laughter].

Gene: She was actually an Osage Indian, she had black hair. She doubled Jane Russell under contract for eight years,

	so you know she was well-endowed. I went to Korea with her on a USO tour and I went with her for a few years.
JF:	I won't take you down that road.
Gene:	You can, I've had twelve wives and she was one of my favorites. She was just a great gal.
JF:	Well, on the set of *Honey West*, you were introduced to Anne Francis. Tell me, what struck you about her?
Gene:	What struck me about Anne Francis? Well, I used to, at that age, read *Playboy Magazine* and I'd see all those pretty girls. And then I saw Anne Francis–and I said she's ten times better-looking than any of those girls. I said she's the prettiest woman I've ever seen in my life. And when she came up to me, she gave me kiss right on the mouth. Oh, she must have been teasing or something. A great personality. I don't know why she did it; I just remember the room starting to go around and I said, "I'm in love." As pretty as she was–as pretty as she is–she's twice as much of a woman, class-wise. Somebody that is with you and talks to you, and makes you feel like you're an equal. That isn't easy with a lot of people. This town–it's changed. Years ago at the studios it was wonderful. Now it's become a little bit bloodthirsty. But I've got a lot of good friends, among my closest friends are in the movie business, mostly stunt men, directors, producers, actors, and actresses.
JF:	Now, one of the things that *Honey West* is known for is that sometimes the fight scenes would be a close-up of Anne grabbing somebody, and then they cut to a long shot of a guy with a wig and with high heels on. Was that you?
Gene:	No, I stopped wearing high heels years ago because I

sprained my ankle in them. Now I should start wearing them again because of California mixed marriages. I'm glad my wife is in the other room.

JF: [Laughter].

Gene: I used to double for women; I doubled women for years and years because they weren't that tough. Then it came down that you couldn't double women, they had to get women. The only time you could double a woman is when they couldn't find a woman to do it. Now you also cannot double blacks–I did a lot of that, Spanish and everything. I am Osage Indian, I can do Indians and I was born in Guadalajara, Mexico, so I can do Spanish guys. I've done a little bit of everything.

JF: Describe to me, if you can, as stunt coordinator, what you did on *Honey West* as there were a lot of fight scenes in this show.

Gene: Yeah, I set up a lot of the fights and you have to do it so that they're safe. Take two, take three, take four, so they don't get hurt. Then, in case I'd forget, I'd go home to my wife and fight a little bit to get the feeling of realism. I believe if you save yourself one embarrassing situation because you know how to take care of yourself it's worth all the time and effort you put into it. That's why I can take care of myself; I carry a .357 magnum.

JF: Oh, *Dirty Harry*.

Gene: Just kidding. Dirty Harry has beaten me up a bunch of times. Clint has beaten me up in a lot of films–he's an athlete. But back to Anne Francis.

JF: Well, did she work closely with you physically? Did you

	train her in any way? She's a frisky New Yorker, she isn't afraid of anything.
Gene:	Tell me about it. Well, look at me. My nose is under my left eye. Well, when I met her it was right in the middle of my head. She gave me a couple of what-fours and she's tough. I don't know if she's smarter, nicer, tougher, or the prettiest gal I ever met. And, as we would say in wrestling, she's a champion on and off the mat–or on and off the screen. I've worked with hundreds of actresses, and a lot of them are in love with themselves. And I know when they are in love with themselves because I've been in love with myself for years–and I know the difference. Next time I fall in love with myself I'm going to get a younger body. You know, in all the people I've met, and I've met some real nice women, and a lot of them have come down to the gym and worked out, but Anne was the nicest. We respected her and on the set, no hassles. You have a couple of stars working and they argue back and forth who's going to do this, who's going to do that. But everybody was like a family there.
JF:	According to Anne, they were working 60 hours a week sometimes.
Gene:	Well, I was fourteen at the time, so it didn't bother me. But we had some long days. To tell you the truth, after eight hours you get overtime. Four hours overtime for the stuntman doubles his pay. You know something, John, a guy that enjoys his work never goes to work. And I would work for free if I liked the situation; I have helped people out on different shows for free. You know, when you have a sixteen-hour day, it's tough on the actress because she has to remember her lines and then she goes

	into another scene and has to remember other lines. But Anne had total recall–every scene she's in she's happier than a pig in slop–although a lot better looking.
JF:	[Laughter]
Gene:	And I stood there, on one of my first days working with her, and I watch them put on make-up. And I said, "My, God leave her alone! You're going to make her ugly!" She was pretty without make-up.
JF:	If you can recall, what's the funniest thing that ever happened to you on the set of *Honey West*? Or was it just a job?
Gene:	Every time you do stunts, and you're a stunt coordinator or a stunt man, and you create a stunt that goes over well, that's satisfaction. It makes you proud. You know you've done something. If you have an eight-to-five job turning a wrench at General Motors or something, year after year, there's no sense of accomplishment. No pride of ownership. In the movies, if you did a good work, you get an Academy Award nomination. Or a [Golden] Globe award, or anything that says, "This is the best." Of course, Anne was the best, no matter if it was comedy or drama; she did everything like she was born into it.
JF:	Would you say that the best compliment you could say to Anne is that she made it look so easy?
Gene:	You could say she made it look easy. When you're a pro, and she's about as pro as you can get, you expect the best, but you're still surprised when they so something that makes you go "Wow!" She'd be in a dramatic scene,

then there'll be a few jokes, and the switch, like turning a light switch. And it always amazed me because she an actress or actor, and I've done a lot of acting parts–I've been arrested three times for over-acting–

JF: Was the first one at your wedding?

Gene: Eh, which one? Which wedding?

JF: Well, what did you think of John Ericson?

Gene: A wonderful guy.

JF: He did a number of tremendous fight scenes. It looked like they were trading real punches.

Gene: They weren't real punches. My wife and I throw real punches. That's why I'm 'punchy.' Ericson was a good athlete and a real nice guy. A tremendous actor.

JF: I'll give you his address.

Gene: I'd like his address, but I'm married. As a matter of fact, I've had women double me. But that's neither here nor there–a lot of good memories. When I had this roast and Anne showed up after I had not seen her in so long–I was in love all over again. I said, 'How come I look so old and you stopped?' And she's still so beautiful. She looked like she was 30 years old. Well, I took care of myself but I look like warmed-over death.

JF: Tell me about Sharon Lucas. She never got any credit for the series and she's very hard to research. Did you coach her during those fight scenes?

Gene: Oh, yes, Sharon actually was my girlfriend for a lot of years and she taught me trick riding and jumping horses and taught me how to go over the low and high hurdles. When the world record for women was 10:2, she did a 9:8! People don't believe it but she raced a couple of stuntmen on the set and beat them fairly handily. She was a freak as far as athletes go, after playing golf for one year she shot in the high 70s. And she could hit a golf ball 275 yards, which is pretty good. I can't even see that far. At the time she was the most famous stuntwoman, she and her sister Shirley, who's still around and lives in a big ranch up in Rough and Ready, California. But Sharon had a couple of bad falls and, the average stuntman, according to the Screen Actors Guild, lives to be 55. So I've outlived it, I'm fifty-six now! Sharon Lucas also wrestled with me–when I say wrestle I mean judo–she could beat the average man. She'd get down and dirty, you know.

JF: So all those throws on *Honey West* were real?

Gene: Of course she did, if you see any judo throws or any wrestling throws, anything Sharon did she did well. She was good at whatever she did. In the movies, you've got to take a little bit of liberties. Like, if you're a fighter professionally, you don't telegraph. John Wayne would telegraph. He'd throw a punch from leftfield and people could read it and understand it. So some of the things that are really practical, like getting in close and taking an eye out, it doesn't show for the movies.

JF: So how closely did you work with Sharon on these stunt scenes?

Gene: You'd have to be on the set when they're doing things, but she was good enough that, if I weren't there, she could handle the situation. Extremely talented, they just don't make them that way anymore. Anything that she'd picked up was natural–she could chop down a tree, ride a bucking horse, she was a beautiful, beautiful women. Sharon was a hero of mine. She doubled stars in everything, from *Annie Get Your Gun* to *Paint Your Wagon* and she did all these stunts. When she worked, you knew a great job was going to be done because she was a man in a woman's body as far as athletics go! An Osage Indian from Oklahoma. A legitimate Indian and not like these guys selling cigars on the corners from central casting. She was a wonderful person–I mean, I saw her do vaults on horses that men couldn't do. Anything that she tried, she'd pick it up. She was a workaholic and the bad thing is she took care of her mother. Her mother was a nice lady but she smoked–and I've got allergies. And she'd sit down in my house and burn a hole in the chair. I probably would have married her if it weren't for her mother. But a wonderful, wonderful person. And, this is corny, if you lay down with dogs you get up with fleas. And if I socialize with anybody, they'd better be friends of mine. They better be somebody I respect.

JF: You are not one to mince your words, I take it.

Gene: You know, if a person says you're honest, and everybody says they're honest ... I've never written a bad check. I've never intentionally cheated anyone or stole anything. Maybe I have to live with myself. And when I die I've got an eight-to-five chance of going to Heaven because if the good Lord thinks I've done a good job, I'll go there. If he doesn't–I never liked him anyway.

JF: Finally, is there anything about *Honey West* that stands out in your mind?

Gene: John Ericson was a beautiful person to work with.

JF: And you liked Anne Francis?

Gene: It's not that I liked her, I loved her, I respected her. Certain people are heroes. Like when you work with a thousand different actors and some of them, I wonder where they come from. I could tell you about directors that I never respected, a lot of actresses that were always "I-I-I-Me-Me-Me." So when you meet someone like Anne Francis, you've met the best.

Bibliography

LeBell, Gene. *The Godfather of Grappling: "Judo" Gene LeBell, the Only Authorized Biography.* Santa Monica, Calif.: LeBell Enterprises, 2004.

Contact

Gene LeBell
5638 Lankershim Blvd.
North Hollywood, CA 91601-1722
www.GeneLeBell.com
www.ValleyMartialArtsSupply.com

Irene Hervey

LITTLE-REMEMBERED TODAY, Irene Hervey was a glamorous leading lady of B movies of the 1930s and 1940s. She was born Beulah Irene Herwick, on July 11, 1909, in Venice, California, the daughter of a sign painter. Hervey married as musician while still a teenager and divorced four years later, keeping the custody of their infant daughter. Endowed with a dimpled and intrinsically cute demeanor, she passed the MGM screen test upon the urging of a friend and landed her first role in the King Vidor's *The Stranger's Return* (1933). In 1936 she switched over to Universal Pictures. That year she also met and married her second husband, singer and actor Allan Jones, and their son, noted singer Jack Jones, was born in 1938. The following year she accepted what was arguably her most noted role, in *Destry Rides Again* (1939), as an upright irl who steals the sheriff (Jimmy Stewart) from a risqué saloon singer (Marlene Dietrich). Unfortunately, Hervey's career was sidelined by a disastrous car accident in 1943, whereby she retired from the industry for five years. She resumed work in 1949 opposite William Powell in the film *Mr. Peabody and the Mermaid*, where her penchant for elegant sophistication once again manifested. Several more films in supporting parts ensued until the early 1950s, when Hervey deftly transferred to a new medium, television. She consequently landed meatier, memorable, and prolific roles in such fare as *Public Defender, Playhouse 90, The Donna Reed*

Show, *Peter Gunn*, *Perry Mason*, *Dr. Kildare*, *My Three Sons* (nominated for an Emmy) and *Honey West*, among others. Her final two outings on the silver screen were in *Cactus Flower* (1969) with Goldie Hawn and *Play Misty for Me* (1971) with Clint Eastwood. Hervey retired from the business shortly afterwards to work at the Valley Oaks Travel Agency in Sherman Oaks, California, although she came out of retirement in appear in the 1981 TV film *Goliath Awaits*. A dependable performer who invariably imparted great charm to her roles, Hervey died in Woodland Hills, Los Angeles, on December 20, 1998, at the age of 89. She is honored by a star of the Hollywood Walk of Fame.

Hervey's casting as wealthy bon vivant Aunt Meg in *Honey West* was a relative footnote to her long career. She only appeared in eleven episodes and was constrained mostly in the role of comic relief. Her principal-and invariable—activity here was in refereeing Anne Francis and John Ericson during several of their sparring sessions. When allowed some dialogue, she came across as suitably ditzy and likeable in her appointed role, although such casting did not allow for any character development. It is unlikely that Hervey would have been retained had *Honey West* been renewed for a second season but, to the extent scripting allowed it, her trademark charm and sophistication are welcome additions to the show.

Bibliography

McClure, Arthur F., and Ken D. Jones. *Star Quality: Screen Actors from the Golden Age of Films*. South Brunswick, N.J.: A. S. Barnes, 1974.

Seymour, Blackie. "Pentagram Profiles: Irene Hervey: Sparkling with Class." *Classic Images* No. 290 (August 1999): 5-7.

Sharon Lucas

And now for credit where it is *long* overdue. Sharon Elese Lucas was born in Bartlesville, Oklahoma, on June 2, 1928, and subsequently relocated with her family to Southern California. She was part Osage Indian, as was her sister, Shirley, and the two developed a keen interest in horsemanship while in their teens. Both became adept at trick riding and performed at numerous rodeos, including the Denver Grand National, the San Francisco Cow Palace, and similar events in Salinas, Red Bluff, and Palm Springs, California. Sharon matured into a willowy and vivacious brunette, whose attractive looks deceptively masked her phenomenal athletic prowess. By the 1950s she had parleyed her equestrian skills into a career as a Hollywood stunt woman. In this capacity she doubled for such noted actresses as Jane Russell and Marilyn Monroe, and proved no slouch when it came to taking falls from horses, stairs, and the like. According to her sister Shirley, Sharon was routinely challenged by stuntmen to footraces on the set, and invariably beat them. By the 1960s she had emerged as one of the industry's premier stunt women, and excelled at handling two- and four-horse teams, cars and, interestingly enough, fight scenes. Her talents also extended to singing, drawing, sewing, and decorating, in all of which she distinguished herself. Sharon was also an animal lover, exhibited a wonderful rapport with them, and was adept at working alongside a wide variety of birds, dogs, cats, horses, and other four-legged denizens of the movie lot. Such was her renown that on July 22, 1958, she appeared as a contestant on the TV show *To Tell the Truth*.

Sharon's talent reached new heights in 1965 when she was signed to double for Anne Francis in *Honey West*. Because the main character was supposedly adept at martial arts, she studied judo and karate under judo expert/stunt coordinator Gene LeBell, whom she also dated, and flourished in the role. As a series, *Honey West* is replete with violent physical confrontations, expertly and impressively nuanced by Sharon. The donnybrook in the episode "The Gray Lady" is nothing short of breathtaking. The only shortcoming worth mentioning in these scenes was that horrible blonde wig Sharon wore–it flopped about like it was stapled on! After the series ended, Sharon resumed working in motion pictures until 1969, when she was severely injured in a fall during *Paint Your Wagon*. She was forced into retirement and spent the rest of her life in the Penn Valley, California, catering to her two nieces and several horses. Sharon Lucas, stunt woman extraordinaire, died at Spring Manor Convalescent Hospital in Grass Valley on January 24, 2006. She is survived by her sister, Shirley, who also doubled for Anne Francis, and on television shows like *Gilligan's Island*.

www.rodeotrickriders.com/Lucas

Bruce the Ocelot

PETS SPEAK VOLUMES as to their owner's disposition, so it is only natural that a character exuding such feline attributes as Honey West would opt for something like an ocelot. This animal, dubbed Bruce Biteabit by those working with him, has a relative minor role in each episode, yet he acquired an association with the program that is best described as iconic. Ocelots (*Leopardus pardalis*) are, in fact, beautiful creatures and worthy of note. Five recognized subspecies are native to the New World and their range extends from South America up through southern Texas. Appearance-wise, they are appreciably larger than domestic cats, being rather long-legged and (like most small members of Felidae) primarily nocturnal hunters. This fact is underscored by large, oversized eyes that human observers find so striking. Their dappled fur coat is also deemed extremely attractive despite the fact that it functions as camouflage while the cat reposes in thickets during daylight hours. Ocelots are also solitary by nature and males are highly territorial, fighting to the death to defend their turf against interlopers. Sadly, the very appeal of ocelots has made them desirable—not as pets—but rather as *pelts*, and the creature has been hunted into near extinction at several locales. In 1969, 133,069 skins were marketed in the United States alone. A related animal that sometimes substituted for Bruce was the margay, essentially a slightly smaller, thinner version of its famous cousin. It also differs from ocelots by being arboreal (tree dwelling) and is the only member of the cat family capable of descending from trees head-first in squirrel-like fashion. Like ocelots, margays are treasured for their fur and their conservation status is considered guarded. Fortunately, it is illegal to hunt either species in the United States and small colonies still flourish in southern Texas.

Ocelots and margays are wild animals, so their grasp of domesticity remains distinctly problematic. Charming and affectionate as kittens, they enjoy considerable novelty as pets in the United States and celebrities, such as noted artist Salvador Dali, owned them to enhance their status. Adult cats, however, exhibit unpredictably aggressive behavior consistent with an alpha predator from this size range. On *Honey West*, Bruce was played by several female animals (one was actually named Honey) and a margay or two, each beset with its own snarling screen persona. Animal lover Anne Francis bore the full brunt of their erratic disposition by periodically being swatted, scratched, and, in some instances, bitten by her co-star! On several occasions she required tetanus shots following a "too-close" encounter with one of many "Bruces" in the show. The animals in question were provided to Four Star by Hollywood trainer Bruce Helfer, who said, "Our cats were good as long as you didn't push them. They were a lot like a cheetah, absolute dolls to be around, sweet and loveable, but if they don't want to do anything, they won't do it." (*TV Pets*, 139). So, while Bruce may have accentuated Honey's ultra-mod lifestyle and even symbolized her own tigerish sexuality, it promulgated an erroneous impression that ocelots make ideal pets. They do not—and ought to be left alone in the wilderness that spawned them.

Bibliography

Beck, Ken, and Jim Clark. *The Encyclopedia of TV Pets*. Nashville, Tenn.: Rutledge Hill Press, 2002.

Wilsdon, Christina. "A Spot for the Ocelot." *National Geographic World* No. 226 (June 1994): 15-19.

Young, Diane. "The World's Most Beautiful Cat." *Southern Living* 32, no. 10 (October 1998): 130-134.

A. C. Shelby Cobra 289

AN INSEPARABLE COMPONENT of Honey West's free-wheeling and far-ranging aura is her 1965 Cobra roadster, a vehicle that is legendary in the automotive racing world. The firm Autocarriers (or A.C.) of Thames-Ditton (Surrey), England, had been founded in 1907, and by the late 1950s they were successfully constructing a small racing coupe called the Ace. Enter Carroll Shelby, a strapping Texas and former racing car driver seeking to build a lightweight sports car with European flair for the expanding American market. He contacted A.C. in 1961 with the backing of Ford, who also sought a competitor to the famous Chevrolet Corvette, and a year later the new Shelby Cobra debuted with a relatively small 260-cubic-inch engine. Due to its smart looks and good performance, Shelby began manufacturing them in handfuls at his Santa Fe Springs, California, assembly line as A.C. shipped each body and chassis to him. Seeking greater speed, in 1964 Shelby outfitted the Cobra with a large 289-cubic-inch V-8 engine with phenomenal results. The upgraded design reached 60 miles per hour in only 5.5 seconds and covered a quarter mile in 13.9. Thus, the Cobra entered automotive racing history as the world's fastest-accelerating car in its class and was increasingly seen at racing events, especially in the United States. Its name recognition was such that in 1964 the Ripcords recorded their hit single "Hey, Little Cobra." In 1967, Shelby achieved a life-long quest when a highly-modified Cobra hardtop finally defeated the long-victorious Ferrari GTO in Europe. However, sales of the car, while steady, were never sufficiently large to sustain the company, so Shelby quit manufacturing them shortly afterwards. Replicas of this classic hybrid racing machine, a deft combination of British engineering and American power, are still custom-manufactured by Autokraft of Surrey, England, who employ many of the original jigs used on Shelby's masterwork.

The "Wimbledon White" Cobra, No. CSX2540, is featured in a handful of *Honey West* episodes and, in true spy fare, is outfitted with a mobile telephone. The episode "The Abominable Snowman" has the most fun depiction of the car in action, whereby our heroine races down the winding road from Griffith Observatory in pursuit of a baddie. The segment is expertly created from a combination of long shots and tight close-ups with Honey's hair flying in the breeze and blue eyes blazing as she doggedly tails her adversary. In "The Flame and the Pussycat," she is slugged over the head and placed unconscious in the car trunk with the engine still running. The heavy then attaches a hose from the exhaust pipe to the trunk, aiming to asphyxiate her – fortunately, Honey awakens and uses her tire jack to pop open the door at the last moment. Curiously, when the character Honey West is introduced in the *Burke's Law* episode, the exotic car in question driven by Sam Bolt is another British import, the legendary Jaguar XKE. Honey is filmed driving this same car in the pilot episode, "The Gray Lady." Shelby apparently lent the Cobra to Four Star for the rest of the production, feeling that it was useful free publicity. Next to Bruce the ocelot, the Cobra 289 remains the best-remembered iconic representation of *Honey West*; the original vehicle survives today in the hands of Joyce Yates, of Nashville, Indiana, a private collector.

Bibliography

Ethan, Eric. *Cobras*. Milwaukee, Wisc.: Gareth Stevens, 1998.

Friedman, Dave. *Cobra: The Shelby American Original Archives, 1962-1965*. St. Paul, Minn.: Motorbooks International, 2002.

Shoen, Michael L. *The Cobra-Ferrari Wars, 1963-1965*. Vancouver, Washington: CFW, 1990.

www.thecarsource.com

Synopses

"Who Killed the Jackpot?"
(Aired April 21, 1965)

Starring: Gene Barry (Amos Burke), Regis Toomey (Lester Hart), Gary Conway (Tim Tilson), Leon Lontoc (Henry), George Nader (Chris Maitland), Gordon Doversola (Judo man), Jan Sterling, Nancy Gates, Louis Hayward, Steve Forrest.

Script: Gwen Bagni and Paul Dubov

Directed by: Richard Kinon

When revelers at the seedy Queen Hotel discover a corpse draped over a neon sign, Captain Amos Burke, Homicide Division, arrives to investigate. The victim is Andrew J. Selby, a wealthy banker who apparently had no business being where he was, let alone dying there. A preliminary sweep of the crime scene reveals little, and Burke and his two companions are about to depart when he espies a beautiful young woman outside, apparently entering the building. He watches her knock on the door of Selby's room and enter, then waves his friends off and moves in to investigate. The stranger suddenly pulls a gun and declares herself a private investigator, which Burke instantly deduces must be Honey West, a female gumshoe of some repute. "I wondered when we'd cross," she remarks. "So, you're Burke." After Honey mentions that Selby was a client of hers and that he summoned her to the hotel, Burke, unconvinced, cordially "invites" her downtown to issue a full report. "Are you taking me in?" Honey intones. "Is that an invitation?" Burke replies. "Don't let it go to your head!" she quips. The couple depart in Burke's Rolls-Royce, all the while tailed by a Jaguar XKE with Sam Bolt at the wheel. A bout of quasi-playful bantering ensues, whereby Burke delicately threatens to revoke her license for withholding evidence. The two nevertheless enjoy dinner together and Honey is allowed to drive off with Sam on the condition that she drop the case. Back at her office, Honey encounters Chris Maitland, Selby's attorney and a personal friend, who likewise advises her to quit while she's still ahead. She also receives a threatening message on her answering machine, "Honey West, be smart, stay alive–forget about Selby!" Far from intimidated, her interest in Selby's murder is peaked.

The next day Honey initiates a series of encounters by running into Burke at Police Headquarters, and subsequently seems one step ahead of him. Detective Les Hart is smitten by the comely P.I., at which point Burke orders him to tail her–he gladly obliges. Sam also discovers that Selby had been liquidating his assets recently and was carrying $100,000 in a black bag at the time of his murder. Honey tries unsuccessfully to interview Mrs. Vera Selby, a drunken former showgirl, and annoyingly runs head-long into Burke. "I'm leaving now," she yells to Detective Hart, parked smilingly behind her. Honey next collides with Burke outside the residence of Elizabeth Friendly, Selby's secretary and another possible suspect–and absconds with his appointment book before the police can. Back at her office, Maitland yells, "What are we going to plead? Kleptomania?" An angry Burke also arrives outside to recover the address book and Honey quickly dons a geeky brunette wig and costume, slips past the police in Sam's TV repair truck, and makes for the docks of Los Angeles.

There she tries to charter *The Harem*, a rundown boat operated by an equally derelict Stacey Blackwell, who is listed in the appointment book. Honey tries renting his vessel but Blackwell plays coy until she baits him by stating that she was recommend by Selby. Somewhat alarmed, Blackwell invites her into the cabin, then notices that a tuft of Honey's blonde hair protrudes from her brunette wig. He then aggressively comes on to Honey, at which point she chops him into unconsciousness. Honey then flees–running headlong into Burke again—and surrenders her latest clue, a piece of paper with a telephone number. Burke, noticing Sam's electronically-rigged truck nearby, calmly declares, "It's not admissible in court." Honey shoots back, "It helps to get there!" and stomps off toward a payphone. The plot thickens when Honey calls the number obtained from Blackwell, which turns out to be the hotel where Selby was murdered. Suddenly, Mrs. Selby pulls up to the dock in her limo and berates Blackwell as Honey and Sam listen in electronically. Blackwell, growing suspicious of their vehicle, walks up to investigate and the duo roars off in a hasty retreat. "There are *other* characters in Selby's appointment book," she slyly notes.

The pair next shows up at the establishment of Jocko Creighton who runs a dockside marine repair shop. Creighton, a self-styled playboy, claims he met Selby at the bank for a loan and was turned down. He also declares that Selby wanted him to make a pass at his wife to establish grounds for divorce but he refused. "Have you seen Mrs. Selby?" he laughs. "Look, I've got style ... if I wanted to go that route, I've got my pick." "I think I'm getting sea sick," Honey blurts out. Creighton offers to tell her more, but motions toward Sam and says, "Lose the five o'clock shadow, baby, then come back." "Don't shave it too close," Sam fires back. They leave just as Burke himself pulls up to question Creighton. Honey again returns to Blackwell's boat for more answers, only to find him stabbed to death. A subsequent interview with Mrs. Friendly uncovers nothing but additional motives, at which point Sam and Maitland conspire to force Honey off the case before she becomes the next victim. She quickly out-foxes both men, locks them in her office, then makes for Creighton's shop. There, it finally dawns on her that Creighton double-crossed Selby, killed him to take the money, and also murdered Blackwell to remove all witnesses. "You know, I really think that Mr. Selby's little black bag full of money is around here somewhere," she mockingly states. "Why don't I call Amos Burke and you can tell him about it." Creighton, realizing that the game is up, suddenly attacks Honey–who promptly flips him over. Recovering, he grabs Honey as she runs out the door and the two struggle until she elbows him in the ribs, dropping him a second time. Creighton again struggles back on his feet and pursues her out the doorway—when there is a loud "sock" and he comes flying back onto the floor. Captain Burke, who delivered the punch, strides triumphantly in the hallway to arrest him. The episode ends at a swank nightclub where Burke, Sam, and Maitland intensely vie for Honey's attention on the dance floor. Burke wins the final round yet jokingly warns her not to fly too close to the ground lest he clip her wings. Honey, as usual, takes everything in stride. "So...you're Burke," she coos as they mingle. "So...you're West," he whispers low.

HONEY WEST

"The Swingin' Mrs. Jones"

(Aired September 17, 1965)

Starring: Ray Danton (Sonny), Winnie Coffin (Masseuse/Ma), Marvin Brody (Mr. Steele), Louise Arthur, David Armstrong (man), Joel Lawrence, Dan Gazzanga

Script: Gwen Bagni, Paul Dubov

Directed by: Paul Wendkos

The scene opens in a darkened alley where Honey West, disguised as an elderly, rich widow, cautiously walks down to meet a group of blackmailers. There she exchanges $50,000 for a "compromising" photo negative of her. Suddenly, a quick judo flip drops the nearest goon, then Honey pulls her .38 and forces the two remaining men back against the building, assuring them that "company will be here soon." However, she fails to notice that Sonny, the handsome ringleader, is ducked in a building entrance and he promptly slugs her from behind with his pistol. Honey collapses and the thieves escape with their loot just as Sam Bolt pulls up in a car. He dashes over to help muttering, "You and your ideas!" "No postmortems," she retorts, "just help me up." The two then stagger back to the car and inform the real Mrs. Mainwaring that their scheme has failed, and that her $50,000 is lost. Their aristocratic client accepts defeat gracefully, bemoaning the fact that she allowed herself to be seduced and photographed by a young suitor in a hotel room. Honey and Sam, embarrassed by their gaff, encourage Mrs. Mainwaring not to give up. "Give us a little time," Sam assures her. "We'll do our best." "We've already done our worst," Honey chides in. Suddenly, she notices a matchbox cover recovered from the alley belonging to the Royal Manor, an established hideaway for swingers. In a flash the duo determine to lay their snare. "Dust off the expense account, Sam, we're going on a little vacation!" she declares.

The next day heads turn as Honey checks in at the Royal Manor, masquerading as the ultra-fashionable "Mr. E. C. Jones of Beverly Hills." As anticipated, she catches the ambitious eyes of Sonny, lurking about for his latest victim. Honey makes known her wealth, loneliness, and availability to her masseuse, unaware that she is actually Sonny's mother and head of the blackmailing operation. Fortunately, Sam is also prowling about the premises as "Touch Carsteds," a rambunctious playboy with a decided weakness for the ladies. Their reveries are shaken when a man is found dead at the hotel, ostensibly from an accident, but Honey recognizes him as one of the thieves she confronted in the alley. "They play for keeps, Sam," she observes. "They killed him." Sonny wastes no time getting acquainted with "Mrs. Jones," who feigns embarrassment over the recent advances and rejection from "Touch." Recognizing a golden opportunity for blackmail, Sonny broaches the subject with Sam and he agrees to arrange a little "photo session" of him and Mrs. Jones for a cut of this latest $50,000 set-up. Sonny has no idea that Honey, having planted a microphone disguised as an olive in Sam's martini, is listening intently. Sam agrees to the scheme, which quickly goes astray when Mr. Steele, a private investigator hired by Sonny to confirm their intended victim's wealth, recognizes her as Honey West. Sonny angrily declares that "things are going to get a lot hotter," and informs his mother. Sonny, Steele, and the others declare that quitting now would be the better option, but steely old Ma overrules them and decides that Sam and Honey already know too much. Moreover, she insists that their murder be arranged not at the hotel, but rather her own house. When the gang protests the plan she declares, "Now, Sonny, I know you'll do what Mother says."

That evening, Sonny reveals to Sam that the faux shoot is planned at another location, then gives him the keys to his car and the location. Sam and Honey reluctantly drive off as instructed, all the while questioning why the photo shoot is not at the hotel. Honey then asks Sam to kill the motor and, coasting along, she hears the engine of a car trailing them with its lights out. She gets out and approaches the driver, whom she recognizes as one of the hotel employees, and promptly flips him over. Sam arrives as back up and forces him to divulge the location of the others before cuffing him. "You know, Sam, you do that just like in the movies!" Honey exclaims, and the two continue to their rendezvous. Once at the house, Sonny wastes no time taking Honey prisoner at gunpoint while Sam parks the car, but she ignites her exploding earrings and escapes just as Sam charges and the duo quickly subdue the villains. The story ends with Sam and Honey trading judo flips back at her swank apartment, whereupon Aunt Meg appears and states she is lunching with a grateful Mrs. Manwaring. The judo session ends and, once Sam leaves to work on the truck, Aunt Meg gently admonishes Honey by insisting she has to "let the man win once in a while." Honey, having sustained a heavy fall, limps over to the couch and groans, "Believe me, Aunt Meg, you are looking at a sore loser!"

"The Owl and the Eye"

(Aired September 24, 1965)

Starring: Richard Loo (Tog), Lloyd Bochner (Guy Patterson), William Bramley (George Mortimer), John McLiam (Gordon), Guy Lee (Houseboy)

Script: William Bast

Directed by: Paul Wendkos

A svelte, black-clad figure slowly lowers herself on a rope from the roof of the posh and darkened Hirschfield Museum at night. Honey West immediately makes for a display containing a rare and valuable Ming dynasty jade owl. The object is deftly removed and replaced with a fake, then she makes her way back to the rope to depart. Suddenly, the night watchman approaches and Honey ducks into a darkened crevice as he scans the room and its treasures with his flashlight. Fortunately, he soon departs and Honey, clapping her hands, signals for the rope to be lowered again. She stealthily exits herself, owl in hand. Later that night she and Sam return to the museum, negotiate their way past a trio of snarling Dobermans, and present the owl to a very surprised Guy Patterson, the artifact's owner. "We stole it from the Hirschfield Museum...we thought you might like it back," she declares. Both Patterson and Mr. Gordon, the museum owner, agree that the Hirschfield's security measures are inadequate. Rather than face a loss of insurance coverage, both men agree to install an anti-burglar system, invented by Sam, which employs low-level radiation to trip the alarm. They also suggest installing a hidden 16mm camera in the wall, focused on the display case, to record any suspicious onlookers. The scheme appears so foolproof and Patterson is so impressed that he feels that he "owes something" to Honey and asks her out to dinner the following night. Honey agrees and departs but Patterson, getting into his car, is accosted by Tog, a sinister Asian smuggler who insists that the Ming owl be delivered to him within 48 hours.

Back at the office, Honey and Sam watch film secretly taken of George Mortimer, a known importer-exporter from Hong Kong. Sam decides to investigate his room at the Gotham while Honey enjoys a lovely evening with Patterson. Her suitor slyly declares that he will be relocating to Hong Kong, to which Honey comments, "That's a long way to go for a fortune cookie." Worse, his best kiss only rebounds off Honey, who ducks inside her apartment noting, "It's been a lovely tour of the Orient, Guy." The next morning she is awakened by a frantic Sam, who brings headlines announcing the owl's theft. They end up back at the Hirschfield, distressed to learn that the burglar system had disastrously failed–foiled by residue from the owl's own radioactive base. Mr. Gordon is appreciably livid over believing their "hare-brained scheme." An embarrassed Honey declares, "Mr. Gordon, I promise you, we'll bring that owl back to roost!" Sam next comes up with miniature radiation detectors that buzz when tripped, and he determines to revisit the Gotham Hotel and exhume Mortimer's room for the owl. He discovers traces of radiation but no owl, and is then surprised at gunpoint by Mortimer himself. Meanwhile, Honey uncovers that the seemingly wealthy Patterson is actually broke and saddled by gambling debts. She also notes that he attended Harvard and has a degree in nuclear physics, which would account for how he could outfox their burglar alarm. Intent on pursuing her lead, Honey calls and makes a purring pitch for another "date" to learn more. Aunt Meg walks in the room, overhears the conversation, and gets an immediate wrong impression. "Got to get dressed!" Honey exclaims. "Why bother?" Meg quips. The date unfolds charmingly until Patterson is summoned outside by Tog, and she ducks behind the curtains. Patterson and Tog return, at which point the owl is exchanged for $500,000–then Honey's radiation-detecting buzzer inadvertently goes off revealing her real intentions. An angry Tog then pulls out a tranquilizer gun used for his Dobermans, chops Patterson, and shoots Honey into a coma.

Honey awakens onboard Tog's boat as a captive, while Sam, disguised as a sailor, comes aboard looking for her. She places a frantic call for help on her lipstick transmitter, which reveals Sam's identity to the crew. They pounce on him as she breaks a window to escape and is confronted by the three chained Dobermans. She notices the box containing the owl and makes off with it as Tog gives the dogs samples of her perfume and orders them on the chase. Honey is cornered on the deck by the snarling pack and defeats them by spraying the deck with a fire extinguisher, but accidentally drops the owl overboard. Tog also appears and attacks, but Honey disposes of him with a chop and a kick. Her perfume bottle, carried in Tog's breast pocket, shatters and drenches him—and the dogs now chase a new target. Meanwhile, Honey vaults overboard to secure the box, only to find Mortimer swimming away with it, and she attacks. Sam also jumps in, calls on Honey to stop, and declares him to be an ally. It turns out Mortimer is a Federal customs agent who had been trailing Tog for some time. The scene ends with the master smuggler clambering up the boat's mast, cornered by his own Dobermans. A drenched Honey smilingly admits, "It looks like Tog is going to the dogs!"

"The Abominable Snowman"

(Aired October 1, 1965)

Starring: Henry Jones (Reedy Comfort), Barry Kelley (Lieut. Stone), George Keymas (killer), Leon Askin (The Count), Henry Hunter (Lucas), Phil Arnold (Boyle)

Script: Gwen Bagni, Paul Dubov

Directed by: Paul Wendkos

A sleek, white Shelby Cobra pulls into the Griffith Observatory parking lot and out steps Honey West hoisting a salesman's sample case. She hands it off to Mr. Lucas, her client, and wishes him luck at the upcoming novelty show in San Diego. As he drives off a black sedan roars out of the lot in pursuit. Honey immediately gives chase down the winding road and tries to block the assailant, but she is run off the road. Mr. Lucas, meanwhile, hits a road block and crashes down the hillside. Honey stops and dashes over to the site to examine the fatally injured Lucas who is muttering, "Snowman ... Snowman ..." before expiring. She then notices that he is holding a snowman paperweight in his hand, removes it, and hastily departs just as the sinister assailant arrives and begins gathering up various paperweights tossed around the ground. Honey phones Sam from her car and informs him that their client is dead. Back at the office, a distrustful Lieutenant Stone sternly reminds Honey and Sam that their license is imperiled if they withhold any evidence related to this case. "When your father had the agency I never had any trouble," he growls. "I know," Honey fires back, "he used to say how cooperative you were, too." Stone demands to know where the sample case is, but Honey pleads ignorance. Additional threats ensue, so Honey gives Stone a description of the assailant and his license place. He departs and Sam slyly inquires what Honey did with the sample case. "I give you my word, Sam, I did not take that sample case," she innocently declares. "What did you take...?" he inquires. Honey produces one of the paperweights from her pocketbook and Sam flies into a tirade over hiding evidence. "I didn't lie, Sam, he only asked me if I took the case." More screaming ensues as Honey luxuriates in her bubble bath and Aunt Meg placidly knits away. "What are you knitting for her—a straitjacket?" Sam yells. "For me," Meg declares. "Earmuffs."

The pair subsequently learn that the chase car was stolen—and there is no trade show in San Diego—so they determine to follow up. Honey's first stop is the Comfort Novelty Company, which distributes the paperweights. All the while Sam is shadowed on the outside while the assailant enters and shadows Honey. The company owner, Reedy Comfort, cordially checks the item, stating that the snowman paperweight was probably made overseas. Honey then gives him her business card—and he compliments her on being such a pretty investigator. "Mr. Comfort," she purrs, "that's exactly what you are, a comfort...." Across the street Sam is attacked and beats off his opponent. Honey is likewise accosted in the elevator by the sinister stranger, who pulls a gun and demands the "Snowman." A fight ensues and Honey drops him and runs. The two compare notes back at the office and Sam learns that the chauffeur who jumped him has a Swiss passport and driver's license. Honey, meanwhile, bemoans the fact that the paperweight broke and dumped white powder all over her new purse. "Did you have to use evidence as a weapon?" Sam sarcastically notes. "*Where* were you?" she fires back. Honey tries to fix her smeared lipstick when some powder gets on her lip and numbs it. The two immediately deduce that the "snow" in question is actually cocaine—and that they are dealing with a narcotics ring.

Their next stop is the annual charity ball given by the wealthy Count Ioupesecu. Sam disguises himself as a waiter while Honey dons a brunette wig and an atrocious French accent. He thinks the whole idea is ridiculous. Still, she feels that the imported items, the Swiss chauffeur, and a wealthy European count all fall in place together somehow. "Come on, the Count comes here every year to throw a charity ball!" Sam reminds her. "Maybe he throws snowballs as well," she quips. Before leaving, Honey takes a panicky phone call from Mr. Comfort, who claims that people are out to kill him. She allows him to take refuge in her office under the watchful eyes of Bruce the ocelot and proceeds to the party. The sinister buyer immediately sees through her disguise, asks her to dance, and forces Honey upstairs. "I liked you better without the wig," he snarls. They no sooner reach the balcony than Sam conks him out. Honey strongly suggests that he call the police while she ventures upstairs to search for the sample case. Sam protests as usual but, behind his back, she shimmies up an outside lattice to the second floor. Honey finds the sample case and is further surprised to learn that the wheelchair-bound count is indeed behind the drug ring. Honey quickly disposes of him and his chauffeur, grabs the display case, and dashes for the door, but is stopped by Mr. Reedy, gun drawn. "The Snowman" regrets having to shoot Honey but Sam, climbing up the lattice-now sporting a black eye from an encounter outside—intervenes at the last moment and saves her. Honey then calls the police— pausing only to slug a recovering thug ("Excuse me!?")—and asks for Lieutenant Stone. Back at the office, Sam gingerly nurses his shiner with a steak, which Honey removes to cook for Bruce. When he angrily demands to know if the ocelot is more important than him, she smiles and exclaims, "Why, Sam, you're both wild!"

"A Matter of Wife and Death"

(Aired October 8, 1965)

Starring: Dianne Foster (Maggie), Michael Fox (Lieut. Kovacs), James Best, Henry Beckman (Cody), Henry Brandon (Alexander Sebastian).

Script: Tony Barrett

Directed by: John Florea

Sam Bolt pulls up to the beach in his TV repair van, parks, sets up his listening device, and sweeps the bay with binoculars until he finds a small craft with Honey West tanning herself on the deck. Smiling, he contacts her by radio and warns, "You'll get freckles that way-any problems?" "Only a peeping Sam," Honey retorts. "Girl watch on your own time." She is subsequently joined by Maggie, her client, who fears that someone is out to kill her. As the two repose, a skin diver suddenly places an explosive charge on the side of the boat. A vigilant Honey catches the action and orders Maggie to jump overboard at once. The two dive in and the boat suddenly explodes with Sam watching in trepidation from the shore. Back at the office, the duo is grilled by police Lieutenant Kovacs, who warns them that if Maggie gets hurt the police will take the fall. Sam reassures him that all is well and Kovacs, unconvinced, angrily storms out. Honey, meanwhile, hurries back to Maggie's apartment, where she has just received a threatening note under the door. "He never mentioned money," Honey observes," it's got to come up hate, a grudge of some kind." At this juncture, Vince Zales enters and has Maggie sign an insurance affidavit to cover his boat. The phone also rings, Honey answers and encounters Alex Sebastian, Maggie's ex. Maggie talks with him cordially, makes a luncheon date, and dismisses any notion that he is behind recent events. Meanwhile, Sam is outside and espies a stranger lurking near the house, confronts him, and he suddenly escapes in a car. Honey then decides to interview Mr. Sebastian, who is involved in the import/export trade, who relates woes about his junior partner, Frank Webb. "Are you painting Mr. Webb as a suspect?" she asks. "In broad strokes, dear lady," Web asserts. "He's a very violent man." Honey then informs him that Webb died a month earlier and, when Sebastian is not looking, she plants a miniature TV eye in his living room. Sam watches the screen from outside as Sebastian is suddenly confronted in his home by a skin diver, who kills him with a spear gun. Arriving on the scene, Sam struggles with the intruder, who escapes, leaving behind only a valve from his diver's mask.

Honey next pulls up to Maggie's apartment and observes that she is docking her boat alone, then carries a large container into her car. Her curiosity peaked, she steals on board the craft and discovers a diver's suit in the cabin. Sam also returns to Maggie's building, finds the stranger lurking there again, and subdues him in a stiff fight. The seaman is Fred M. Cody, who explains under duress that he did not kill Sebastian. "Watch me convince the lieutenant!" Sam warns, demanding to know more. Cody spills his guts, exposes Sebastian as a diamond smuggler with a foolproof drop-off system. Cody freely admits that he made the drops. "Maggie know anything about it?" Sam inquires. Cody laughs. "Are you kidding, she laid the whole thing out–she was the brains!" Furthermore, when Maggie found out that Webb was cheating on her, she made the last drop herself–a million dollars in diamonds–and nobody knows where. Sam intuitively decides to investigate Vince Zales, who, it turns out, was a former naval frogman who now rents boats. Vince recognizes the face-plate valve as an older model and Sam leaves, convinced he is onto something.

Vince, thoroughly alarmed, calls Maggie and fears they have been uncovered. Sam tunes in electronically to the room outside and hears how the two decide to meet. Vince then drives off with Sam trailing him in the truck. Once at the dock, Vince clambers onto Maggie's boat, where she convinces him that this is their last drop.

Meanwhile, Sam steals onto the boat and hides as Vince suits up and prepares to dive overboard. He is increasingly nervous but Maggie calms him. "Just one more dive, then it will all be over. Then it will just be you and me, and a million in diamonds," she assures him. "What about the two killings?" Vince inquires. Maggie assures him that there was no other way and he jumps over and swims to the drop point. Maggie suddenly hears a loud thud behind the closet, pulls her gun, and opens the door. Out steps Honey who mutters, "Next time I'll try first class." "What next time?" Maggie menacingly notes. Honey reveals that she knows Maggie made the last drop, and that hiring her as a client was iron-clad proof that someone was trying to kill her. The newspaper headlines of her attempted murder also brought Sebastian into the picture, where Vince could kill him. "What's going to happen when he can't find that little box?" Honey inquires. "Oh, he'll find one," "Maggie states, "but it will make a very loud noise." She is apparently willing to kill Vince to keep the diamonds to herself. Sam suddenly distracts Maggie and Honey chops her down and seizes the gun. He then dives in the water trying to warn Vince not to go near the box but an underwater explosion signals that it is too late. "Sam, are you all right?" Honey frantically asks. "I wouldn't know until I take inventory," he replies. Back at the office, Sam and Honey prepare for a night on the town, while Aunt Meg notices that Bruce the ocelot has been licking her jar of vanishing cream. He then mysteriously ducks out of view and Aunt Meg questions if he really has "vanished." After some frantic searching, Honey points out that the cat is up in the closet, his face covered in vanishing cream. "Bruce, honestly," she muses, "you can't change spots on ocelots."

"Live a Little...Kill a Little"

(Aired October 15, 1965)

Starring: Warren Stevens (Arthur Strickland), Harry Millard (Charles French/Margardo), Herb Edelman (Phil Moody), Mary Murphy (Vicky), Maurine Dawson (Karen French)

Script: Tony Barrett

Directed by: Murray Golden

A tall, comely girl strides out of a decrepit dance hall at night and is jostled by drunken revelers. Wrenching herself free, she continues down the street until she hears a voice call her name from a parked car. It's Honey West, who says, "Don't be afraid, I just want to talk to you." Suddenly, Honey notices the unmistakable sound of a rifle being cocked and sees a sniper on the roof top aiming at Karen. "Karen, get back!" Honey yells as she flashes a portable flood lamp from her car and shines it in his eyes. The assassin loses balance and falls from the roof as pandemonium breaks out below. Karen then bolts from the scene and catches a cab, which is immediately tailed by a dark sedan as the police arrive. Having lost her mark, Honey calls her partner on the phone. "Sam, when I got up this morning I felt something was going to go wrong. It sure did!" Back at the office, Sam begins screaming at her for taking on a dangerous assignment without consulting him. Honey brushes off the criticism, and continues rearranging her flowers. "I am not shouting!" Sam screams. "Then why are you turning purple?" she inquires. Honey calmly explains that their new client is Arthur Strickland, whom Sam recognizes as one of the nation's top tax attorneys. It seems that the sister of one of Strickland's associates, Charles French, has gone underground to escape a jealous ex-boyfriend. "They know she's in Los Angeles and they want her found. We got the job!" Honey exults, "And there, oh masculine one, you have all of it–every syllable." Honey subsequently pays a visit to Arthur Strickland to further clarify things and she encounters Charles French, Karen's brother, who has just arrived from San Francisco. Honey nonetheless threatens to drop the case. "I was hired to find a missing girl and I found her–but I ran into World War III." Sam is outside, eavesdropping intently, when he is slugged from behind. Meanwhile, Strickland insists that he told Honey the truth, save for one fact. "Now's the time," she insists. Strickland candidly admits that the man Karen is running from is manically jealous and has promised to kill her. He asks her to continue on the case for the girl's sake—and Honey reluctantly agrees.

Back at the office, Honey applies a bandage to an injured Sam, insisting, "You certainly are grumpy!" She also caught a glimpse of the man who conked Sam, heavyset at six-foot, three inches. The dead sniper is the only lead they have. Honey offers to go downtown to investigate the identity of the sniper—but Sam adamantly refuses. "Oh, no, you stay right here!" "You're so masterful!" she sarcastically blurts. "And don't con me, Honey. " No, Sam..." "No, I mean it—from now on we're going to have a new system around here." "Yes, Sam!" From now on we're going to do things in a sensible, orderly way." "Yes, Sam!" "From now on you are not going to do any more crazy things!" "Right, Sam!" The scene then cuts to Honey working in a cheap dance hall downtown. Her next partner turns out to be Sam, who berates her for ignoring sound advice. "Do you have to chew that gum," he growls. "When in Rome," Honey replies. "You know, you're a kook," he insists. "Oh, Sam," she replies, "don't get purple all over again." Honey also promises to pump Vicky, a friend of Karen's, for information. Vicky insists Karen was running away from something, then espies Honey's Derringer in her purse–and kicks her out. Vicky then calls her boyfriend–as Sam is outside taping–but "Phil" hangs up.

Back in the office, Sam and Honey track down the phone number, which belongs to Phil Moody, a hulking, freelance private investigator with a reputation for working both sides of the law. "Could he be the fellow that bounced you around in that truck?" she asks. Sam immediately makes for Moody's office where he uncovers clippings that reveal how Charles French is actually Charles Margardo, a well-known gambling figure with syndicate connections. Meanwhile, Honey tails Phil Moody to a darkened street and watches as a car pulls up, then the driver gets out and apparently knifes him. Before dying, Moody blurts out Karen's address as "110 Malibu Heights"–and Honey takes off. She cautiously enters the apartment and approaches Karen, but is suddenly surprised by Charles, gun drawn, who takes both women off at gunpoint. They are subsequently bound in Strickland's cellar and Karen confesses to Honey that Margardo, her ex-boyfriend, is part of the syndicate, and that she knows a lot of names. Moreover, she is scheduled to appear before the crime commissions, which makes her a threat as long as she is alive. "I should have asked for more money...," Honey groans. Meanwhile, Sam arrives outside Strictland's house as Margardo begins planning to drop both women into the sea from his boat. Strictland, however, does not want to know the details and, furthermore, questions the wisdom of killing Moody. "Don't you know anything about people?" Margardo states. "A buck-hungry eye who recognizes Karen and then sells her out to me–he deserves to die!" Suddenly, the horn on Margardo's car starts blowing and the two hoods run outside–where Sam is waiting, and he captures both. Back in the cellar, the hostages are freed but Margardo pulls a gun and prepares to escape. Honey promptly chops the weapon from his hand and Sam battles him to a successful finish. Honey, realizing how perilously close to death she was, inquires, "Sam, how did you know where to find me?" "Simple, this was the only place left to look." "You're wonderful!" she beams. Back at the office, Sam and Honey are dressed and going to do the town, but he takes Bruce's favorite security blanket from him. "Sam, you're secure enough," she remonstrates. "Let Bruce live a little!"

"Whatever Lola Wants..."

(Aired October 22, 1965)

Starring: Audrey Christie (Lola Getz), Johnny Haymer (Emanuel Rodriguez), Horst Ebersberg (Gunter), Richard Angarola (Ramon Vargas/Raul Lukas), Don Gazzaniga (butler), Jerry Brutsche (Carlos)

Script: William Bast

Directed by: John Peyser

A frightened man huddles against a wall as Ramon Vargas, a Latin-American underworld figure, pulls a knife and chases him down a fire escape. Pausing to jump, he hesitates a moment too long and Vargas throws the knife directly into his back. He then tosses the body over the railing and into a garbage container just as the collection truck hoists it overhead. Meanwhile, Honey West arrives outside the building, catches the elevator, and knocks on a prospective client's door. It is opened by none other than Vargas himself, who entreats Honey to help him snare a Mr. Rodriguez, the man who swindled his brother out of a large fortune in South America: all she has to do is attend a charity ball given by Lola Getz ("The Hostess with the Mostess"), wait until the suspect–who has a fondness for beautiful women–approaches her, then find out where he is going. Cautious but intrigued, Honey agrees to take on the case. Back at the office, a concerned Sam demonstrates a poison gas pen and a necklace that functions as a microphone. "What could happen at a charity ball?" she asks. "With me not in there you'll think of something!" he insists. The next evening Honey arrives decked out in her elegant black gown and makes a favorable impression on Lola, the host. At length she introduces her to Rodriguez, a charming man who is smitten by this winsome guest. After dancing, the two step out onto the balcony and into the moonlight. "With you I am inspired," Rodriguez tells her, and proposes that they fly to Paris for a romantic interlude. "It's so sudden," Honey says, feigning indecision, and momentarily departs to contemplate their tryst. Rodriguez then summons his German accomplice, Gunter, who recognizes Vargas as Raul Lukas, a fugitive criminal. It turns out that the dance was a ploy of theirs to lure "Vargas" to the party where he could be killed. Upstairs, Honey contacts Sam on the microphone and says, "We got what we came for, Rodriguez is on his way to Paris. Now we can collect our fee from Vargas." Suddenly, she notices that the two hoods are abducting Vargas into a room beneath the stairs and she follows to rescue him. Sam, listening from outside, tells her, "I think you better get out of there, this wasn't part of the deal,"— but she refuses to abandon her client. Honey continues searching near a large mirror, reciting "Mirror, mirror, on the wall..." when Lola, gun drawn, suddenly steps up from behind murmuring, "Who's the nosiest one of all!"

Honey ends up in a cell with Vargas, who confesses he was a racing syndicate fixer and previously the Number 2 man in all South America until he decided to "go solo." He then feigned his own death in a plane crash, and continued winning every race fixed by the syndicate. His only contact, a jockey named Carlos, died in "a bad fall–a fatal one." Honey then suggests that they get out immediately and she concocts a scheme. When Vargas suddenly summons the guard to check out an unconscious Honey, she promptly sprays him with her gas pen. The two dash back to the top floor, and run headlong into Lola and Rodriguez. "Double, double, toil and trouble," she cackles. "You should have know you can't beat the syndicate!" Gunther also mockingly declares that "Carlos" was part of their snare, and when Vargas killed him for passing false information, they knew he was coming to contact Rodriguez. The two are taken down the stairs again, where Lola reveals the extent of her operations–a room filled with computers, telephone banks, and several operators. "What are the odds on the race to Mars?" Honey intones. "I like your style, Honey," Lola laughs, "It's too bad you're running on the wrong track." As Honey and Vargas are being put in boxes for a flight to Caracas, Honey screams into her mike, "Help somebody, anybody!"— and Lola deduces that she must have a partner. Sam, now alerted, overhears that Gunther is coming out to the car to kill him and lays in wait.

At the limo, Gunther is dispatched with a single punch and Sam dons his white jacket to pass as a butler. Once inside, he moves around to the room under the stairs and is surprised by Rodriguez, whom he slugs and then takes him and Lola hostage. "All right, where is she?" he demands, and is told at the loading dock downstairs. The three return to the party, at which point Lola tosses a drink into the air, rolls under the table, and pandemonium ensues. As bodyguards close in, Sam shoots out the lights to escape and, once outside, notices a truck speeding away down the driveway. He jumps on the roof, then grabs the steering wheel, forcing it to crash. Sam has no difficulty subduing the two men, while Honey works herself free and restrains Lola as police sirens begin wailing in the distance. A subdued Lola dejectedly asks for her mink stole and, while opening up her make-up kit, suddenly throws a switch on it. "Well, it's goodbye to the sweetest racket in the Western Hemisphere!" she shouts as her mansion explodes. An incredulous Honey remarks, "I'll say one thing for you, Lola—your party did turn out to be a real blast." Back at the office, Sam, in a mocking impression of Rodriguez, kisses Honey's hand, claims to be inspired, and wants to do something "wild." "Paris, Sam?" she inquires. No—he has a hamburger joint in mind. "All right, so call me basic," Sam says with a laugh. "All right, Basic," she fires back, "I'll get my hat."

"The Princess and the Paupers"

(Aired October 29, 1965)

Starring: Michael J. Pollard (Jingles), Philip Ober (J. J. Vanderhyden), Nino Candido (Marv), Stanley Adams (Tobias Quinn), Don Gazzanica (first man), Joe Perry (second man), Bern Hoffman (steam fitter), Richard Crane (master of ceremonies), Bobby Sherman (Nicky Vanderhyden).

Script: Leonard Stadd

Directed by: Virgil W. Vogel

A new rock group, The Paupers, finishes playing at a swinging dance club to rounds of applause. Returning backstage, the three members are accosted by two hoods who enter their room, kidnap member Nicky Van, and beat up band mates Jingles and Marv. A ransom note is then affixed to a guitar addressed to millionaire J. J. Vanderhyden, and then they depart. Mr. Vanderhyden subsequently informs Honey and Sam that Nicky Van is actually his son, Nicky Vanderhyden. Worse, the kidnappers are demanding $100,000, and warn them not to call the police. "I'm not at all sure you'll recognize my son from this picture," he states, giving Marv and Jingles a hard look. "The last time I saw Nicky he'd seems to have taken on the color of his surroundings!" He also informs that Nicky's manager,

Tobias Quinn, recently wanted Mr. Vanderhyden to front money for a Pauper promotional album. Rather than wait to hear from the kidnapper, Honey decides to check out Quinn, a sleazy operator who makes a pass at her. A quick judo hold promptly puts Quinn in his place and he mutters, "A private eye–what a waste!" He also informs Honey that Nicky Van has no talent and Honey assures him that the money will be forthcoming once the promotion budget is shown to Vanderhyden. While Quinn is digging through his files, Honey also places a hidden microphone under his desk. She then assures him, "There's no catch, just give me the facts and figures and if it's not too much of a swindle, I'll tell J.J. to back it." Honey then rendezvouses with Sam in the repair truck, wonders why Quinn has not called Nicky about the promotion, and deduces that he knows nothing about the kidnapping. Back at the office, Honey instructs Aunt Meg to transcribe anything that Quinn says of importance. Suddenly, a call arrives from Vanderhyden: he has just heard from the kidnappers, so Sam and Honey intend to set a snare for them.

Honey sits by a pond surrounded by revelers in bathing suits as Vanderhyden delivers the $100,000 in a thermos jug. She monitors the signal it emits while Sam lurks nearby on a boat, pretending to fish. Suddenly, a scuba diver appears on the shoreline and absconds with the ransom money. Despite Honey's best efforts, he gets away. The jug is then found empty and Sam goes back to check the adjoining woods. A curious onlooker gets uncomfortably friendly with the bikini-clad Honey, who promptly flips him back in the water. Sam, meanwhile, gets hit over the head and collapses. Back at Vanderhyden's, Honey suggests that Quinn is their biggest suspect. "Yes," Vanderhyden notes, "if *he's* the kidnapper." The phone rings and a sinister voice berates the millionaire for bringing private investigators into the scheme. He also informs him that his "package" is waiting for him at the end of Newell Canyon Road. The three quickly drive over to an abandoned cabin, only to find Jingles bound and gagged. Honey also finds a new ransom note thanking them for the "down payment" on Nicky, then adds, "and for a quarter of a million more, we'll send him back alive."

Back at Vanderhyden's, Jingles explains how he was called by Nicky and told where to pick him up–and then was jumped by the same two thugs who abducted him. An angry Sam paces threateningly in the background, insisting that he recount things "slowly and carefully, friend." Marv likewise claims he was nowhere in particular when Nicky phoned. A frustrated Honey exclaims, "Oh, boy, this kidnapping is about as phony as your stories!" Moreover, she deduces that the entire scheme was raise the $100,000 for the promotional record from Nicky's father. "That means the police are going to wonder why the kidnappers didn't ask for a quarter of a million in the first place," she explains. They also tar Quinn as part of the plot, seeing that the ransom amount is identical to what he sought for the recording. "Only something went wrong," Sam snarls. "The police are waiting in the wings." Suddenly, Marv cracks and confesses that it was all Nicky's idea. He also confesses that Nicky hired the hoods to make it look real. "And they found that they were onto a good thing and decided to go into business for themselves," Honey concludes. Jingles also implicates Quinn and Honey goes immediately to his office to confront him. Quinn calmly denies any knowledge of the kidnapping, the two thugs, or the quarter of a million ransom. "You're talking wild!" he insists. She departs, quipping, "I'll let you think it over—maybe your memory will improve." Back at the office, Aunt Meg informs him of Quinn's calls to a "Freddy." She also receives an envelope with money from Vanderhyden, who wants her off the case. An angry Honey storms over to Vanderhyden's place, pleading with him not to trust the criminals. He insists on proceeding and refuses to divulge where the money is going, so Honey "accidentally" dusts the bills with talcum powder as a tracer. Back at the office, Aunt Meg intercepts another message from Quinn that suggests Nicky is at Malibu Canyon, the old Appleby Ranch. "Aren't you going to wait for..?" Meg asks. "Time and tide!" Honey blurts, darting out the door. Reaching the ranch, Honey is quickly accosted by one hood, which she drops, but is knocked out by the second. She awakens bound next to Nicky. "I know you started something that may take the Marines to finish," she scolds him. Honey manages to remove her belt, revealing a concealed penknife. "How come you're carrying a knife?" Nicky asks. "Because I'm a regular cut-up!" she angrily retorts. Suddenly, two shots are fired and both hoods are found dead in the next room. Honey recognizes Tobias Quinn's car pulling out of the ranch. However, back at Vanderhyden's, she correctly deduces that Jingles is the murderer, not Quinn. Honey then offers to check his hands under a ultra-violet light for talcum powder. His charade unveiled, Jingles suddenly bolts for the door. Sam hits him with a tackle and Honey helps subdue him. That evening, Sam, Meg and Honey visit the nightclub where Nicky sings on stage, accompanied by his dancing girlfriend. "I wonder why he doesn't call his act 'The Princess and the Pauper'?" Aunt Meg innocently ponders. "You're the only princess in these parts," Sam tells her with a grin. Honey momentarily feigns jealousy, and then smiles.

"In the Bag"

(Aired November 5, 1965)

Starring: Everett Sloane, Robert Carricart (Arkudion), Gene Darfler (goon), Don Gazzinga (T-Man), James Donahue (Father), Maureen McCormick (Margaret Mary Driscoll), Len Lesser (Mr. Crimm).

Script: Gwen Bagni, Paul Dubov

Directed by: Seymour Robbie

During a transcontinental flight, a little girl accosts several passengers exclaiming, "She's a monster! All she does is torture Maggie and me!" An irate Honey West steps up behind her, matter-of-factly declaring, "Margaret Mary, it's torture time..," and physically forces her back to her seat. During the struggle, Honey manages to spill the girl's glass of water on a passenger and profusely apologizes. She is naturally relieved once the plane lands and they get off, at which point Margaret Mary warns, "You just wait until I tell my father!" "You do that and I'll charge him double!" Honey fires back. Sam Bolt then steps up to greet them and they continue to the baggage claim area. Meanwhile, the two passengers that Margaret Mary pestered are also awaiting their baggage, when one them, Mr. Arkudian, is suddenly snared by a Treasury Agent. He is escorted off but not before switching his travel bag for Margaret Mary's—which his partner then inadvertently absconds with. The errant child also disappears from sight, panicking Honey and Sam and forcing them to ask airport authorities keep a lookout for her. Back at the office, the two argue heatedly over whether or not to call the police for fear of upsetting the child's parents–then Aunt Meg suggests a truce and that they check the child's flight bag. Both are surprised when shaving implements are found and Honey realizes that the bags were switched at the airport. Suddenly, Bruce the ocelot attacks the shaving brush, breaking it, and valuable jewels spill out. "They're priceless," Aunt Meg gasps. "Emeralds, rubies!" "That's what I call smuggling," Honey cuts in. The door buzzer suddenly rings and the man from the airplane–who identifies himself as Mr. Bartholomew–appears at the door with Margaret Mary and wishes to exchange the child and her flight bag for his. Honey feigns gratitude and offers him an agency pen–with a radio receiver concealed inside–as a token of appreciation.

Sam immediately begins tracking the pen's signal to the downtown area. Meanwhile, in their hotel room, Mr. Arkudion and Mr. Bartholomew–*sans* his heavy make-up and disguise–argue over their misfortune. Arkudion assures his partner that the private investigator would never recognize him now, to which he observes, "But she will recognize *you*, and since we're in this together, that worries me a very great deal." Before leaving, Bartholomew breaks the pen in half and Sam loses the signal. Sam and Honey next return to their office, only to find it has been ransacked. "Looks like the Normandy beachhead!" he quips. Honey rescues Bruce from being wrapped in a curtain, which is stained with blood. Apparently, the cat put up a good fight against whoever did the wrapping. Suddenly, there is a knock at the door and in steps a bespeckled, frightened old man named Mr. Beadie-actually Bartholomew without makeup–who pleads with Honey for help. Beadie explains that his house is haunted and feels that his brother is somehow doing it to have him committed and steal his inheritance. "You must come tonight," he begs, "I can't face another nightmare." An empathetic Honey agrees to help just as Sam calls her and says, "Powder your nose, we're going for a ride–we're getting a signal again!" The two clamber into the truck and trace the signal to the local park–where Margaret Mary is using one of the company pens to draw for Aunt Meg's amusement. A frustrating false alarm.

A discouraged Honey decides to call on Mr. Beadie's "haunted house" that evening. Once inside she is quickly accosted by Bartholomew and Arkudian, who force her to summon Sam by phone. Sam unwittingly agrees to come, complaining that now, somehow, a pen signal he monitors seems to be following *him*. He drives along in the dark, tailed by a sedan driven by the man whom Honey spilled water on in the airplane. Honey, meanwhile, is entrusted to a dim-witted accomplice who constantly complains about a having headache. Playing coy, she gets on her lipstick microphone to alert Sam of the trap. Honey also offers her guard a neck massage, promptly knocks him out, then escapes just as Sam pulls up. Sam is suddenly jumped himself by an unknown assailant, whom he dispenses with one punch, then encounters Honey lurking outside the house. He subsequently enters in the front door while she returns through the back, and they quickly disarm their antagonists. "All right, head 'em up–move 'em out!" she exults. Sam wants to call the Treasury Department just as his unknown assailant suddenly steps in the door declaring, "Save the call!' He introduces himself as Mr. Crimm, a Treasury agent, and produces a badge. Sam apologizes for slugging him and returns his gun. "You will get a special commendation from the Bureau," Crimm states as he scoops the jewels into his pocket. Honey smiles obligingly—then flips Crimm over. "He's no T-man!" she exclaims. "He could have nabbed those two at the airport and he would have used a search warrant on our office. It's a hijack–those scratches on your hand belong to Bruce." Afterwards, Margaret Mary is united with her father, who hopes she was not too much trouble. "Trouble?" Honey coos. "Margaret Mary, for Heaven's sake—she was an absolute angel!" She and Sam then drive off, finally relieved to be free of this troublesome burden. Suddenly, a voice crackles over the radio, "Bye, Uncle Sam! Goodbye, Miss West!" An incredulous Honey declares, "She took my lipstick!"

"The Flame and the Pussycat"

(Aired November 12, 1965)

Starring: Liam Sullivan (Mr. Canby), Sean McClory (Mr. Booth), Harry Baschas (Mr. Flowers), R. J. Nelson (policeman), Ken Lynch (Lieut. Barney).

Script: George Clayton Johnson

Directed by: James Goldstone

A car slowly pulls up in a darkened alleyway and disgorges a figure clad in fireproof clothing. After picking the door lock, he enters a warehouse labeled "Arthur Flowers, Wholesale Drugs" and begins throwing incendiary bomblets at the merchandise. Suddenly, he is ensnared by a net dropped from above as Honey West and Sam Bolt race down a stairway to apprehend him. The figure, however, lobs a bomblet at the pair then escapes through the doorway, locking them in. The scene then switches to police headquarters, where an enraged Lieutenant Barney dresses Sam and Honey down for breaking and entering, among other offenses. Honey reminds him that there have been four warehouse fires in four months and that they were trying to prevent a crime. Barney nonetheless threatens to revoke their license if they incur so much as a parking ticket. We next view Honey's white car-double parked-outside the office of Confederated Insurance Co., where she banters with the firm's chief investigator, a charming Irishman named Mr. Booth. Honey is conducted into the office of Mr. Canby, who knows who she is and refuses to hire her. "Perhaps little girls should stay around the house, don't you think?" Booth chimes in. "Wouldn't that be rather dull for little boys?" comes Honey's riposte. Canby then abruptly dismisses her with a curt, "Good day, Miss West!" "It was when I came in," she mutters while departing. Honey then artfully dodges a parking ticket and heads back to the office. She passes the time throwing darts at a picture of Canby, to which Sam inquires, "Feel better now?" "Not yet," she snaps. "This kind of therapy takes time." Aunt Meg suggests they all cool off at the horse track, but Honey insists on going back to the warehouse and hunting the arsonist, insisting, "Maybe we'll find a hot lead." She next enters the warehouse office and encounters Mr. Flowers, the owner, and offers to solve the case at no charge. Flowers agrees and gives her the key to the warehouse–with Sam listening intently from the truck. No sooner does Honey leave than Flowers makes an urgent phone call to somebody, insisting they have big problems.

When Flowers departs, Sam and Honey re-enter the warehouse and discover that, instead of medical supplies, the "merchandise" in question consists of boxes of old magazines addressed from Dresden Chemicals. Back at the office, Honey phones Booth and warns him that they are paying off phony claims. Unfazed, he invites her to a social engagement which Canby is attending and suggests he inform him there. Honey trots out to her car and gets slugged from behind while getting in. The assailant places her limp figure in the trunk, drives off, parks, then attaches a rubber house from the exhaust pipe. The fumes begin choking Honey who, desperate to escape, ingeniously uses the tire jack to pop open the trunk. Back at the office, Sam scolds her for leaving alone and dresses the big lump on her head. Honey conjectures that somehow Canby and Flowers are connected in the cover up–she somehow needs to connect Canby to Dresden Chemicals and Sam volunteers to have a look at his personal files. Mr. Booth also calls and expresses concern that she didn't pick him up as planned. They both agree to meet at Flowers' warehouse to "snoop around." Honey charges off and tells Aunt Meg to inform Sam where she will be. Meanwhile, Sam is going through the files at Mr. Canby's office when he slugged from behind by Mr. Flowers and knocked out. Flowers then suddenly flees as Canby enters the office, who then promptly calls the police. An infuriated Lieutenant Barney chews Sam out, who tries to explain that they suspect a tie between Canby and Dresden Chemicals

Meanwhile, Honey pulls up in front of Flowers' warehouse as Flowers ducks inside. Drawing her gun, she begins calling for Booth in the darkness, then stumbles into the body of Flowers atop of some crates. Booth's laughter begins echoing through the warehouse and, dressed in his fireproof garb, he suddenly confronts Honey and orders her to drop her gun. Honey instantly deduces that Booth works for Dresden Chemicals and that no medical supplies were ever burned. Booth admits that he collected the insurance money along with considerable profit from real supplies that were sold on the foreign black market. "I know you're busy keeping the home fires burning," Honey blurts out, "so I won't take any more of your time!" Before she can run, Booth tosses a fire bomblet and cuts off her retreat. Honey then retrieves her gun and shoots Booth, only to learn that his outfit is bulletproof. Suddenly, Sam and Lieutenant Barney burst through the door and corner Booth on an overhang. Stymied, Honey suggests that they shoot at his fire bombs as she provides a diversion. As Booth prepares to throw again, Sam and Barney shoot and detonate the device in his hand. He falls from the balcony in a fiery crash as Honey looks on in disgust. The next morning Honey is awakened by Sam who wonders why she is sleeping so late. Aunt Meg also walks in, having won a large sum at the race track. "That beautiful horse paid 100 to one. I really should split it with you, dear," Meg exclaims. "Why?" Honey wearily inquires. "It was his name," Meg announces. "Fire Bomb!"

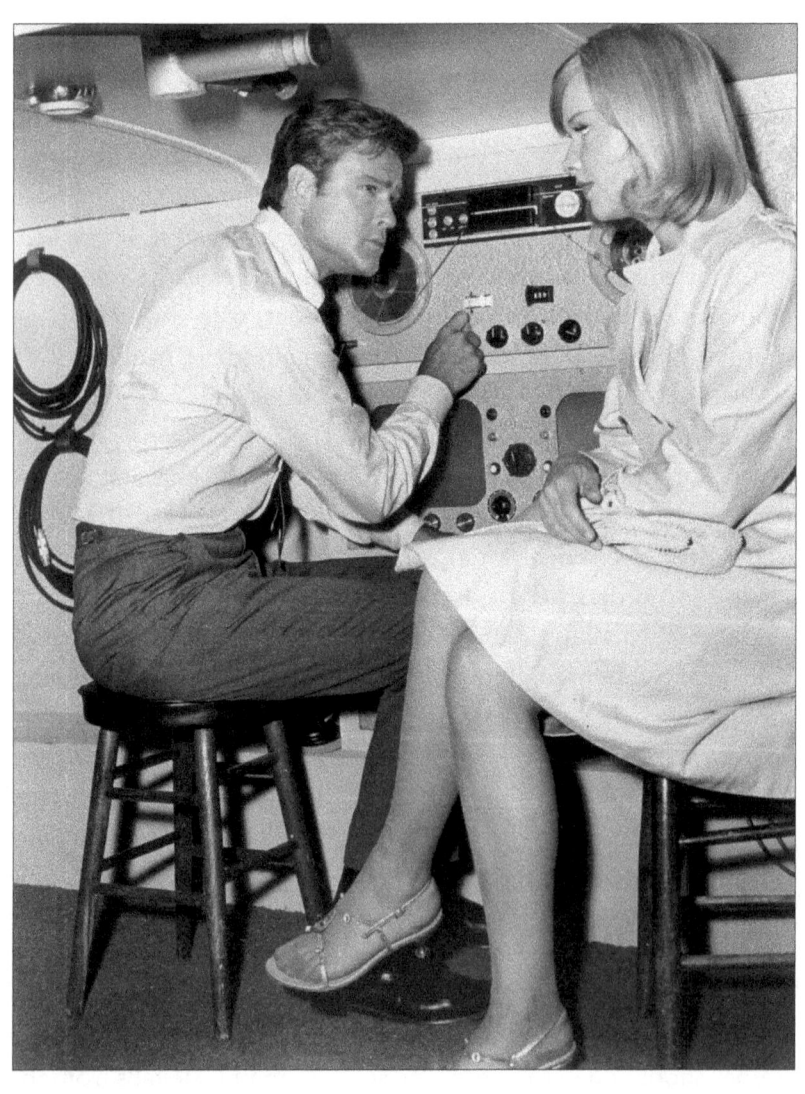

"A Neat Little Package"

(Aired November 19, 1965)

Starring: J. Pat O'Malley (Francis Grady), Arthur Batanides (Chico), Roy Jensen (Ed Stasio), Val Avery (Roger), Sydney Smith (Charles Addison), Harold Fong (custodian), Barbara Morrison (woman), Norman Palmer (customer), Gil Stuart (desk man), Charles Wagenheim (desk clerk), Clarence Klung (Maitre'd)

Script: Gwen Bagni, Paul Dubov

Directed by: Murray Golden

"Mrs. Grady," a comely blonde, enters a seedy downtown hotel and approaches the front desk. After being grilled by a skeptical clerk, she is allowed to go to room 318 to meet her "husband." The woman is Honey West, hot on the trail of her latest ne'er-do-well. Just as she departs the clerk calls ahead and notifies the room's occupant to expect company. Honey no sooner enters than she is greeted by a man seated, with his gun drawn. "You can call me Roger," he says. "Must I?" she replies. Several quick chops ensue, the man drops, and Honey escapes down the hall. Pausing only to open the stairwell door, she darts onto the fire escape and waits for Roger and his accomplice to take the bait. Once downstairs, the two men realize they have been outfoxed and run outside to check in back. "Sam, I'm trapped in the alley," Honey says into her microphone-ring. "Better back the truck in all the way!" Sam instantly complies and the thugs question why he is there. No sooner does one check the back of the van than Sam conks one guy out while Honey kicks the other on his backside. "All right, Sam wagons west!" she shouts as Sam peels away. Back at the office Sam and Honey begin questioning Francis O'Grady, a local newspaper vendor, and demand that he tell them the truth as what gives. After a few moments of soul searching, O'Grady confesses that he has temporary amnesia from a recent car accident and cannot account for a new $100 bill in his pocket, the room key to the hotel, and, worse—a big bundle of $150,000 wrapped in newspaper that he knows nothing about. "I don't know the truth," he pleads. "That's the frightening part. I lost my memory!" Honey and Sam agree to help. Donning glasses, Sam reopens O'Grady's newsstand and he begins bantering with customers as Honey watches from the truck. "No rise out of anybody," he complains by radio. "This is a cold lead." "We'll stay 'till it freezes over," Honey curtly reminds him. Suddenly, Honey spots Roger the hood, who gets in a car and drives off. She follows in close pursuit and ends up at a Polynesian restaurant. The custodian directs her to Mr. Chico's office, but Honey withdraws. Meanwhile, Sam runs into one irate customer, suspects a connection, and photographs him with his watch-camera. He turns out to be Charles Addison, an important figure in the construction business. "How does he fit in with a package of money wrapped in newspapers and two gunsels in a cheap hotel?" Sam ponders. Honey knows one way to find out.

 Attired in a dark wig and tight Asian garb, Honey successfully applies for a job at the restaurant and a very appreciative Mr. Chico makes a pass—which she ducks. Back at the office, O'Grady suddenly remembers that it was Addison who gave him the hotel key–and the package. Sam and Honey determine to find out why and visit Addison's luxury hotel. Approaching the elevator they observe one of the hoods walking away. "How does he tie in with a man like Addison," Honey ponders. The duo proceeds to his room, which is unlocked, only to find him drown in the bathtub. Back at the office, Honey dresses for her job at the restaurant, insisting, "Well, if there is a tiger in your hokey jungle this could be the bait to make him roar," she quips. "Yeah," Sam blurts, "or put him in the mood to kill." Unfazed, she intends to lure the culprits out with Sam's photo of Mr. Addison. At work, Honey delivers the photo to Mr. Chico, which elicits a strong reaction–as she suspected it would. Chico then sends for Roger and tosses Honey out of the office. Tippy-toeing around, she leans next to the window and overhears Chico talking to Ed Stasio, a dangerous underworld lone shark, on the intercom. He fears that their connection to Addison is being uncovered. Sam, eavesdropping electronically, entreats Honey to get out of danger, but she determines to find Stasio and heads back. She next runs headlong into Roger, who corners her. Once again, she dispatches him with some well-placed chops, then ties him up. Continuing back into the restaurant, Honey is taken hostage by Chico and a stooge. "Take off the wig!" Chico demands. "It keeps me warm," Honey protests. She is then hauled before Mr. Stasio himself, who explains that he loaned Addison $100,000 for a month–with a $50,000 surcharge. When Mr. Grady suddenly disappeared, along with the money, he felt he had no choice but make an example of Addison by drowning him. Stasio then motions for his consorts to take Honey out to the lake. "You do have a thing about water, don't you?" she blurts while being dragged away.

Suddenly, Sam bursts through the office door and momentarily subdues Stasio after a stiff fight. Meanwhile, Honey also dispatches her two opponents while walking down a flight of stairs and an all-out melee ensues in the lake. Honey is nearly drowned but Sam frees her, fists flying, and Stasio is finally subdued. "Well," she exults, "we finally got ourselves that tiger after all, didn't we, Sam!" As the police lead the criminals way, Sam and Honey sit on the stairs, dripping wet, and discuss how to charge Mr. O'Grady for their services. Honey convinces him to charge him only $100—and then nothing at all–to which Sam reluctantly agrees. "What am I going to do with you?" he protests to his pouting lady friend. "Buy me a Polynesian dinner!" she chortles. "I'm hungry after all that swimming."

"A Stitch in Crime"

(Aired November 26, 1965)

Starring: Laurie Main, Charlene Holt (Claudia), James Sikking (Valentine) Herbie Faye (Mr. Kessler), David Pritchard (Frankie), Nino Candido (Buddy), Marjorie Bennett (Ma)

Script: Gwen Bagni, Paul Dubov

Directed by: John Peyser

Honey and Sam are driving north in their van when three rowdies in a white station wagon continually cut them off and harass them. At the time, the duo is transporting a fortune in designer dresses for a client in San Francisco. Honey toys with the idea of withdrawing $1,000 from the company account to buy one, and Sam confesses, "I knew it, when you starting loading those dresses on board, I got those empty bankbook feelings." Honey indignantly reminds him, "At a thousand and up they're not dresses, they're gowns!" Driving ahead, the rowdies return for another swipe at the van. Sam wants to get out and clobber them, but Honey suggests that they break for coffee at a nearby restaurant. While ordering, Honey and Sam are accosted by two rowdies, whom Sam promptly dispatches, and they flee. "Hey, you two got quite an act!" an incredulous store owner exclaims. "We travel, too," Honey states as they walk off. Once outside, they see that their van has been stolen. Later, the police deliver Sam and Honey to the van, now abandoned, and endure some good-natured ribbing from the rural police. The fortune in gowns is also missing. Honey then discovers a clue–a guitar string–hiding it from the police with her foot. The couple drives off and delivers the bad news to Mr. Antoine, who is beside himself in anxiety. Now he only has one gown left for a fashion charity ball that evening. "My chance to crack the international market and you get into a fight with some punks on the highway," he declares, "Those gowns are worth a million dollars in business to me by the end of the year!" Honey determines to help by attending the ball in one of her own gowns. Back at the office, she tells Aunt Meg to pack a thimble, for she'll be going along. "Oh, goody!" Meg chortles. "I get to play, too!" Sam also reveals that the head thug harassing them was Frankie McGovern, a hard-core felon. "Frankie-boy, I hope you're a music lover," he muses.

Sam next checks into Mr. Kessler's music store, where the guitar string was sold, and the owner identifies Frankie and also mentions that he placed a $20 deposit on a guitar that will be picked up that evening. "You don't play the cello?" Mr. Kessler inquires. "With a face like yours you gotta play something." "Yeah," Sam tells him, "a waiting game!" After Frankie arrives that night, Sam tails him closely in the van. Meanwhile, Honey, accompanied by Aunt Meg—posing as a seamstress—arrives at the charity ball. Mr. Antoine introduces her as "Helga" from West Germany, and asks Claudia, his usual model, if she can substitute for her this evening. Claudia agrees—then slyly calls Honey ugly in German while Honey beams and says "Danke!" Honey next dons her gown and when Antoine asks what good all this will do, she responds, "You never know, someone might drop a stitch." Antoine's photographer, Mr. Valentine, takes her picture, then Claudia informs him that "Helga" is a phony. "Well, in this business, she's not alone," he retorts. As Honey struts the catwalk a messenger, whom she recognizes as one of the hijackers, delivers a box to Antoine, then runs. She hastens over and opens it, finding a ruined dress and a ransom note demanding $75,000. Antoine cannot possibly meet their demands, so Honey contacts Sam, now watching a coffeehouse where Frankie darted into. The two then take on beatnik disguises and repose in the coffee house, waiting for something to happen. Honey next espies Mr. Valentine, Antoine's photographer, walking in and he enters a backroom. "Things are coming into focus," she notes. "I have a hunch he's the Pied Piper–there go the rats!" As Valentine and the thugs depart through a back door, Honey resolves to set a snare.

Back at his office, Mr. Antoine informs Valentine that he is going to pay the ransom and that the money is in the office. Honey, who is revealed to him as a private investigator, also requests that he bring his infrared equipment to photograph the thieves during the drop off. She and Antoine depart briefly while Valentine places a desperate call to Claudia and alerts her that their victim has the money. "I love you, darling," Claudia purrs—then hangs up and returns to kissing Frankie. Sam is outside, listening on intently as the hoods call back with instructions to haul the suitcase of money to the corner of Fourth and Park at midnight and drop it at the park bench. Honey smiles and informs Valentine that his part is over and that Mr. Antoine should call the police. She pulls her gun and Valentine grabs it, so she flips him over. That evening Honey makes the drop as scheduled with Sam close by in the van. Once the suitcase is picked up, they tail the hoods to the Metropolitan Cleaning and Drying shop. En route, Honey sheepishly confesses to Sam that "There's 900 dollars of our money on top of those phony bills...." "You didn't tell me that part!" he angrily snaps. The duo park and sneak inside as Honey mutters, "What a perfect place to hide a designer's collection." They finally subdue the three criminals–including Claudia—after a big row and Honey declares, "All right, Sam, gather the clan!" Gazing at the luxurious wardrobe before her, she sighs, gives off a forlorn look, and whimpers, "Finders keepers?" Back at the office, Sam paces nervously as Honey is late getting dressed for the opera. She finally appears resplendently bedecked in her evening finery; Sam gasps in wonderment and the two depart in style. Just at the door, Honey and Aunt Meg shoot glances at each other–then wink.

"A Million Bucks in Anybody's Language"

(December 3, 1965)

Starring: Steve Ihnat, Harry Bellaver (Charles Neeley), Ken Lynch (Lieut. Barney), Sarah Selby (Dora Neeley), Frank Scannell (driver), Percy Helton (Wiley), Judy Kane (Dottie).

Script: Tony Barrett

Directed by: John Florea

One night, while bathing, Honey receives a desperate call from Charles Neeley, a fellow private investigator who mysteriously pleads with her to come to his office. He instructs her not to be seen and to park directly in the garage. She complies and enters his office while, outside, a mysterious figure begins welding something into her Cobra's wheel well. Honey looks around Neeley's office and finds an envelope addressed to her with a $50 bill inside. She then calls Sam, rousing him from a deep sleep, and the two drive over to Neeley's house. There, they apparently observe Charley's car–with him sitting in it. They get out to confront him when the car suddenly explodes, immolating the driver. Back at police headquarters, the duo is grilled by an angry Lieutenant Barney, who bemoans the fact that his only lead is the victim's sister, a local hot dog vendor. Barney also warns them to drop the case, insisting, "Honey, this is police business, now. Charley's dead." Honey, pointing to the envelope, declares, "Charley left us this–Charley is still our client." The two then repair back to Charley's office, which has since been thoroughly ransacked. "Well, so much for leads," Sam sighs. "It's a pretty good lead in itself," Honey notes. "Charley had something that someone wanted." Suddenly a figure begins approaching in the darkness. Sam almost attacks him after he opens the door, but it turns out to be Lieutenant Barney. Barney informs them that Charley's house was also torn up and he also recently stayed with his sister a couple of days–as if he was afraid to go home. A thorough search turns up nothing, but Honey manages to salvage a phone number from a pad. Sam dials and gets the Tiger's Torso, a fancy restaurant on Melrose–again not much of a clue. They return to their own office, which they find totally ransacked. Worse, Aunt Meg is bound and gagged and even Bruce the ocelot has been stuffed in a desk drawer. "Some watch dog you are," Sam exclaims. "Half pussy cat –half chicken!" The two free Aunt Meg, who assures them she is all right and sheepishly admits that she picked the pocket of the thug who tied her up. The wallet belongs to Charley Neeley!

The scene switches to the Tiger's Torso, where Honey, bedecked in a skimpy tiger outfit, works as a waitress. She informs Sam that Mr. Garth, the boss, has handled two drive-up orders personally–and it happens a third time as they speak. Watching from the van, Sam observes Garth hand the driver a small package and then drives off in pursuit. He cuts the driver off, flashes his private investigator's credentials and questions if he is really going to catch a plane. "A boxed lunch on a jet?" he inquires. The driver then panics and drives off, knocking Sam over and spilling the contents of his box – hundreds of British pound sterling notes. Sam takes the money over to Mr. Wiley, a currency expert, who marvels over their accuracy. "Take off your hat, Sam; you're in the presence of genius!" According to Wiley, only one man could manufacture such accurate copies–Walter Miller—an expert printer and plate maker. Back at the Tiger's Torso, Sam informs Honey of the plates and she determines to plant a bug in Mr. Garth's office. "Oh, pussy cat," Sam mockingly leers as he tosses her a quarter tip. "Thanks a lot, Diamond Jim," she replies. Honey plants the bug and is nearly caught by Garth, but escapes by mentioning that a man wanted to see him then took off. Garth is perplexed, but believes her. Sam then interviews Charley's sister, who agrees to let him search her cellar and hands him the key. "How can you help Charley now?" she pleads. "There's someone you don't help," Sam reminds her. "The man who killed your brother."

Back at Tiger's Torso, Honey taps into Garth's phone and hears details about their next drop. "Not here—the other place," an ominous voice growls. Sam, meanwhile, discovers Walter Miller's file stashed behind an old painting—and connects Charley to the counterfeiting plot. Honey, however, is determined to follow Garth to the new drop off—an isolated cabin in the woods. "Honey, will you go home?" he pleads. "Will you for once listen to reason!?" Continuing on, she parks outside the cabin and is quickly accosted and brought before Garth. He offers her $50,000 for the missing plates, but she insists on twice that. Garth orders his henchmen to tie her up, and then Sam suddenly bursts through the door, gun drawn. He orders Honey to be freed, at which point she tells a thug, "You've got some unwrapping to do." A fight erupts as the three hoods try to escape but they go down in a hail of fists, kicks, and chops—then Honey holds them at gunpoint while Sam checks out her car. There he encounters and captures a fourth culprit—who turns out to be Charley Neeley himself. Back at the cabin he confesses he accidentally killed Miller, stole the plates, then faked his own death—using Miller's body—to throw Garth off. "Then you got hungry," Honey sadly notes, "and decided to go into business for yourself." To buy time while he perfected his plans, Charley also admits he welded the five counterfeit plates to Honey's car. "The most valuable car it town," he adds. Honey, shooting a glance at Sam, blurts, *"You* said I paid too much for it." Back at the office, Sam brings Honey a floral arrangement, a gift from Lieutenant Barney. He then gives Aunt Meg a kiss for stealing the clue that helped break the case, and states that Barney wants her to quit picking pockets while she's still ahead. "It's habit forming," Sam warns her. "I expect he's right!' she beams—holding up Sam's wallet!

"The Grey Lady"

(Aired December 10, 1965)

Starring: Kevin McCarthy (Mr. Ivar), Cesare Danova (Abbott), Nancy Kovac (Nicole Predue), Bert Parks (himself), Pat Collins (Babs Ivar), Fred Vincent (Lieut. Keith)

Script: William Link, Richard Levinson

Directed by: Walter Grauman

A posh Los Angeles hotel is the scene of a star-studded reception for French movie starlet Nicole Perdue, who is greeted by an adoring throng and an on-camera interview by emcee Bert Parks. Watching these proceedings from the television in Perdue's hotel suite is Abbott, a suave diamond thief, busily helping himself to her expensive jewel collection. Once finished, he turns out the light and replaces a normal light bulb with one giving off a blinding flash. Suddenly, Honey West emerges from a closet, gun drawn, forcing him to stop. The two exchange some witty repartee until Abbott makes a grab for Honey, whom she adroitly flips over her shoulder. "Never tried to kiss a black belt before," he confesses. "There's a first time for everything," she says smilingly. He then feigns missing a contact lens and asks her to turn on the light while he gropes for it. She inadvertently complies, and is blinded by the flashing bulb. Honey fires her gun in the wrong direction as he slips out the door and heads toward the elevator. Honey gets on her lipstick microphone and alerts Sam Bolt, waiting downstairs, to be on the lookout for the dapper stranger. Unknown to Sam, he is in the elevator changing his appearance. Dressed now as a maintenance man, he completely fools Sam, directs him to the loading dock, then drives off with his stash. Back at the hotel room, the police interview at irate Predue, who hired Honey to apprehend the noted celebrity thief as a publicity stunt. Youthful Lieutenant Keith also berates Honey for not being more careful, at which points she notes that Keith is new on the job and offers to have dinner with him to get professionally acquainted. Sam and Honey then return to their office where he complains about wasting time chasing a jewel thief while other unsolved cases pile up. Honey mentions that the thief gave her a clue about "kissing the lady goodbye," and it just so happens that millionaire New York socialite Babs Ivar is arriving in town with her diamond, "The Grey Lady." She convinces Sam the lead is real. The duo is next at the airport when the bickering Ivars arrive. "Nice couple," Sam notes. "Of what?" Honey shoots back. "Well, the bait's here, let's hope the fish are biting." As they depart, Abbott the jewel arrives on the escalator and, watching the Ivars ride off, smiles broadly.

Honey next drives her Jaguar XKE to the well-heeled West Hollywood district, where she meets with a rather dubious Mr. Ivar. She warns him that a notorious jewel thief is going angling to steal his wife's collection. Ivar, unimpressed, thanks her for her crass offer and brusquely bids her farewell. The scene cuts to a shooting range with Honey angrily blazes away at a target. "I mean, you actually said that to him?" Sam inquires. "He turned a very satisfying shade of magenta!" she responds. Despite the brush off, Honey remains determined to catch the jewel thief–with Sam's unwilling help. At the hotel, she cons him into switching the Ivar's usual TV set for one with a closed-circuit camera inside. "A new kind of set," Sam jests. "It watches *you*!" He returns to the van while Honey remains glued to set and watches Abbott enter the room. Honey removes her formal attire, revealing a form-fitting, black catsuit beneath, and rappels down the side of the building. Once inside Ivar's room, she draws her gun and again surprises the thief as he is admiring the Gray Lady. "We all have our faults," Honey chides him. "Curiosity seems to be one of yours," Abbott growls." It could get you killed one of these days." Honey menacingly raises her gun, declaring, "Better keep your sword dry, mister–this isn't a cigarette lighter I'm holding!"

The impasse ends when an incredulous Mr. Ivar suddenly opens the door and sees the pair. He feigns surprise as Honey explains the set up, then suddenly chops the gun from her hand and pulls his own. "You jackass!" he tells the thief. "Everything we worked on and planned on you let a girl blow it all!" Honey quickly deduces that Ivar is up to an insurance scam, whereby Abbott steals the jewels and he cashes in on the policy. "A setup," she exclaims. "The old insurance game and I was dumb enough to fall for it." Ivar also announces that he found Sam outside in the van, monitoring the television, and conveniently "disposed" of him. "Your friend will have quite a headache in the morning," he says with a grin. Ivar then orders Abbott to eliminate Honey, when she mentions that the "Gray Lady" is actually a fake–a fact he will find out when he tries selling it in Mexico. Abbott angrily demands proof that the jewels are real and Ivar shoots him dead. "The best laid plans of mice and men…," a smirking Ivar says. He next trains his gun on Honey and she expertly chops it from his hand. "All right, let's play your game, Miss West," he blurts while removing his jacket. "We are going to have a ball!" Ivar then chops a table in half to demonstrate his own martial prowess and Honey bolts for the door. She is suddenly kicked to the floor and a ferocious hand-to-hand struggle ensues. Honey finally prevails, knocks Ivar out, then leaves–pausing only to brush her hair in the mirror. The next day she drops by the hospital where Sam is nursing a large bump on his head, and tells him that offers are pouring in, thanks to good publicity. "Our phone is ringing like the bells of St. Mary's," she exults. A pretty nurse then enters to change Sam's bandage and Honey smilingly departs, placing a "Do not disturb" sign on the door.

"Invitation to Limbo"

(Aired December 17, 1965)

Starring: Louise Troy (Darlene the Hypnotist), Peter Leeds (Charles Kenyon), Wayne Rogers (murderer), Stacy Harris, Dan Frazier (Harold Sutter), Judy Lanf (Miss Christie), John Launer (Tyler), Lonnie Fotre (Mrs. Tyler), Cal Bolder (motorcycle cop), Will J. White (guard), Danny Reese (juggler).

Script: William Link, Richard Levinson

Directed by: Tom Gries

Charles Kenyon, a distinguished-looking, middle-aged man of some import, enters a guarded business facility. Moving down the corridor he is challenged by security for identification, is cleared, and then proceeds to his office. Once inside, he begins unlocking a secure safe, unfolding valuable plans and starts clandestinely photographing them. All the while his actions are being monitored by Sam Bolt on a closed TV circuit. Suddenly, Honey West steps out from a closet and mockingly begins photographing him. "Are you through with your night work, Mr. Kenyon?" she coyly inquires. The man, trance-like, then turns on Honey and tries to strangle her, but she disposes of him with a few chops. On cue, Sam Bolt rushes from outside, unaware that he himself is being observed by a stranger in a car. Sam and the guard burst in the room but Kenyon, as if waking from a trance, asks Honey who she is. "I'm the girl you just tried to strangle," she muses. The following day, she and Sam appear in the office of Harold Sutter, the manager, and explain that they were secretly hired by his board of directors to catch the thief stealing company secrets. Sutter cannot believe that Kenyon, a trusted employee, would do such a thing. Nor can Honey understand why he was acting drugged or in a trance. He agrees not to notify the police but has to fire him as a security risk. The duo then leave. On the way out, Honey holds up a hidden microphone in front of the secretary, asking, "Do record all your boss's conversations?" "It's company policy," she snootily replies, after which Honey and Sam proceed to the door. Outside, the stranger places a hidden package in the front seat of Honey's car. The duo splits and she drives off alone. However, Honey is pulled over for speeding and when she gets out to sweet-talk the officer from giving her a ticket, a bomb explodes in the front seat. "I forgot my thousand-mile check up!" she tells the incredulous officer.

Back at police headquarters, Lieutenant Sherman examines part of the home-made bomb and asks Honey if anybody is out to kill her. "A couple dozen people, including Sam sometimes," she says. "That would be justifiable homicide!" he angrily blurts back. However, Honey refuses all offers of police protection. Back at their own office, Kenyon shows up and explains he has no history of drug use and does not remember anything. Honey and Sam inquire if he has ever been hypnotized and Kenyon says yes, at a nightclub called the Sandbox. Moreover, he received a special invitation to attend. Honey and Sam show up the next night where Darlene the Hypnotist is entertaining with three businessmen on the stage. Honey learns from the wife of one that her husband, Mr. Tyler, received a special invitation. Sam also observes the stranger snap his fingers after the show and instructs Mr. Tyler, apparently entranced, to show up at a prearranged address. That evening, Honey climbs onto the roof of the building where Mr. Tyler is expected and places a microphone on the skylight. After arriving, Tyler is given instructions to steal plans from his office, photograph them, and deliver the film back to Darlene. He will remember nothing. Honey suddenly stumbles and the noise draws the stranger to the roof, gun drawn. He is about to toss her over when she chops the gun from him and the two struggle. Honey is nearly strangled before Sam scales the ladder clouts him. "Thank you, Sam!" a grateful Honey exclaims.

Downstairs, Sam and Honey accost Darlene and her henchman, making them recant. Impressed, Honey admits, "It was a beautiful gimmick while it lasted–hypnotizing all those businessmen and not one of them remembers a thing about it." Darlene admits that they have never met their employer, that they only drop the film off at a sauna bath, where it's traded for money. "It's like the good little tooth fairy!" Honey notes. She next appears at the sauna and watches the transaction unfold. Wearing only her overcoat, she trails the courier to a greenhouse on the outskirts of town. Honey alerts Sam by phone and, despite entreaties to remain still, she darts into the building. There, Honey is quickly apprehended by Sutter and his secretary at gunpoint. He proudly explains how he sells secret plans to companies around the country by placing the film in potted plants shipped as gifts. "Now what are you going to do now that I've ... er .. caught you with your plants down?" she inquires. Sutter plans to drop her into the ocean and hands his gun to his secretary while he brings the car around. Honey begins powdering her nose with her microphone powder case, which tips Sam and Lieutenant Sherman off as to the goings-on. Sam asks Sherman to hit his siren and it distracts the secretary long enough for Honey to chop her down. Sam and Sherman also race up and Sutter is apprehended. The next evening, Mr. Kenyon takes the duo to dinner and mentions that he received a another special invitation with entertainment. The three attend and watch a fiery juggling act that apparently mesmerizes Sam. "I must admit, though, I like the hypnosis act better," Kenyon confesses. "Me, too," Honey states. "How about you, Sam? ... Sam??" He simply stares off into space.

"Rockabye the Hard Way"

(Aired December 24, 1965)

Starring: Vincent Beck (henchman), Paul Sorensen (Swetlow), Ivan Triesault (Schotze), Larry D. Mann (John Raven), Joe Don Baker (Rocky Hanson), Pepe Calahan (Jose) Gil Lamb (Counterman), Jonathan Hole (chemist), Bella Bruck (Mexican woman).

Script: Gwen Bagni, Paul Dubov

Directed by: Bill Colleran

Honey and Sam pull into a dilapidated Mexican village, looking for a certain Mr. McWherter. The locals seem uncooperative, even fearful, in finding "Senior Mac" until they are directed to a local cantina run by Lazlo Schotze, who assures them that no such person exists. The two then climb up the back of the cantina where Honey observes McWherter being shot and killed by a mysterious, bald-headed man. They run out to the front and enter the room, only to blunder into a roomful of rough-looking men playing cards. Excusing themselves, they return to the street, but Honey is determined to check out McWherter's apartment. Once inside she observes a suitcase full of expensive shorts, a radio transmitter, and is accosted by the bald-headed killer. She disarms him with a chop and barely escapes to Sam in the car, then flees under a hail of bullets. Back across the border, the duo repose at the Circle Cafe with Rocky Hanson, their client, who says that McWherter was his only witness. Honey has him recount his story one last time: Rocky was running a classified trucking job with secret missile parts, he had coffee at the truck stop, drove a few minutes before feeling sleepy and woke up five hours later with a hangover. His rig was thoroughly checked, nothing was touched. His company, Gage Electronics, then fired him for being unreliable. Honey deduces that somebody slipped him a mickey in his coffee and guesses that the perpetrator was fat and bald – like the thug in Mexico. Rocky agrees, and then Honey, looking up at a "'Help Wanted" sign, says, "Sam, it's so nice to be wanted."

Honey is working behind the counter, driving the regulars crazy, when Sam, who also found work as a driver at Gage Electronics, walks up. "Daily runs so my nights are open," he chides her. "But my doors are closed," she responds. The two briefly banter and then go outside to trade notes. Sam declares that he was snooping around McWherter's old locker and found an expensive, custom-made jacket belonging to wealthy socialite John Raven. Honey next appears at Raven's mansion, finds him playing pool, and he invites her to try her hand. She shoots several balls in the side pocket and, intrigued, Raven invites her to dinner that night. "We could have a game," he suggests. "You wouldn't like the way I play," she warns. "I call my own shots." Once Honey departs, Raven's bald assassin enters and admits that he gave the expensive jacket to McWherter as a gift. Raven deduces that it was found at his locker at the plant and that Honey has somebody working at Gage Electronics. "Find him," he snorts, "and we'll bury them both."

Honey and Sam next appear back at Raven's darkened house and artfully steal their way in. Sam protests, "We could get five years for breaking and entering!" "Honey replies, "Don't be silly, Sam, we're not going to break anything." "Very funny," he notes. "You're going laugh us right out of our license." She plants a bug on Raven's phone, and then they observe a door with double locks, open it, and find infrared photographic equipment. Honey postulates that they are spies of some sort, photographing Top Secret missile parts and relaying the information out of Schotze's cantina in Mexico. At that juncture Sam wants to contact the Secret Service, but Honey frowns on the idea for lack of credible evidence. Suddenly, Raven's henchman enters the door—Honey douses the lights and quickly disposes of him; the two then make a hasty exit.

Raven realizes that the duo had been in their house and Sam is fingered at Gage Electronics by his contact there. They then plan a special run for Sam, intending to drug him and kill him on the road. Sam and Honey are outside listening in, and he realizes that he cannot miss the run or Raven would suspect they are on to something. Honey agrees, reassured that she will be working at the café and can switch any drug-laden coffee Sam is offered. Moreover, she appeals to one of her druggist friends, Mr. Brady, for an antidote to counteract any barbiturates he might ingest. Back at the Gage Electronics, shift manager Swetlow informs Sam that he is slated for a special run that night. Sam checks into the café as planned and is suddenly joined by Swetlow for coffee. "Saccharine?" he ask Sam. "No," Honey interjects, "Big Sam thinks he's sweet enough." She then observes Swetlow slipping something into his coffee. Honey accidentally spills the antidote, and is forced to pour Sam's coffee into a thermos to keep him from drinking it. "Drink your coffee, Bolt," Swetlow insists, "before it gets cold." Sam tries, then declares, "It's too hot." He departs as planned, pours his coffee out the window, and then pulls over while being closely tailed by Raven, Swetlow, and his goon. As he feigns unconsciousness, the three enter the truck and begin photographing its contents. Unknown to them, Honey is right behind and closing fast. At a given signal, Sam tosses a flare then he and Honey quickly attack the spies, subduing them. "Quoth the raven, nevermore!" she exults. Back at the café, Sam jealously watches Honey being interviewed by a handsome young Secret Service agent. Rocky is nonetheless grateful for their help. Sam, however, still protests her fawning attention toward the government agent, when she asks, "Are you sure they don't have women in the Secret Service?"—then stuffs a piece of toast in his mouth, silencing him.

"A Nice Little Till to Tap"

(Aired December 31, 1965)

Starring: Anthony Eisley (Peter Sutton), Howard McNear (Mr. Tweedy), Marvin Brody (Mears), Lou Krugman (Durant), William Benedict (Farley), Chuck Hicks (Crowley).

Script: Tony Barrett

Directed by: Jerry Hopper

A black limo drives down a city back street with two nervous passengers inside. One, Peter Sutton, times the exact progress the vehicles make while Mears, the driver, nervously tries to maintain an even pace. "I've got a mother-in-law that does less backseat driving," Mears protests. "Your mother-in-law makes you this kind of money?" Sutton inquires. At length they arrive at their objective, a manhole cover, and stop. Mears inquires how much more time will he have to make the test run, and Sutton insists until he gets it perfect. Watching these proceedings closely is Sam Bolt, shadowing them from behind and electronically eavesdropping. Pulling into a warehouse, Mears asks Sutton how well is he flirting with a bank teller." "Jennifer Tate," Sutton beams. "A real honey." Tate is actually Honey West, impersonating a teller in order to catch a ring of thieves who have been knocking off banks with impunity. Honey wields her usual effect on men, and when an elderly customer winks at her, she feigns surprise and says, "Mr. Schlockenheimer!" The dapper Sutton steps up next, equally smitten, and asks her out for dinner. She agrees and subsequently confesses to Sam by radio that he is so charming, he cannot be a suspect. "Honey, your 'girl' is showing!" he warns. Back at police headquarters, Sam and th lieutenant are grilling Mr. Tweedy, a somewhat detached bank executive, who suspects that his banks have been knocked off with inside information. Honey has staked out the last remaining bank handling industrial payrolls and is waiting at the bank for the master thief, who invariably befriends a teller, to make his move. Regarding Sutton, the lieutenant confesses, "He might be our boy ... or he might just like a pretty face." That evening, Honey and Sutton bear enjoying a night out while Sam, disguised as a waiter, takes a note to him from Mears. He then accidentally spills champagne on the unsuspecting Sutton, while Honey picks his pocket and retrieves the note. It states that Durant is already in town while Crowley, another accomplice, is arriving on a plane from Seattle that evening.

At the airport, Sam accosts Crowley and threatens to take him down to police headquarters, when the suspect suddenly bolts across the street and is struck dead by a car. Sam and the lieutenant then check the dead man's file and learn that he is an explosives expert–just the man needed to knock off a heavy safe. "The best!" the lieutenant declares, "He's opened more boxes than Houdini!" Back at Sutton's apartment, he is still making his play for Honey and she blithely informs him that the bank has $300,000 in the vault for Western Pipe because they make payroll on Monday. Suddenly there is a knock at the door and Mears informs him that "we've got problems." Sutton is forced to dismiss Honey goodnight, admitting to a "business crisis." She feigns indignation stating, "Really? What's her name?" She departs and Sutton is told of Crowley's death, but he angrily declares that he will handle the explosives himself. "*That's* the pigeon from the bank?" Durant laughingly inquires—then informs him that his "girlfriend" is actually Honey West, a private eye. He recognizes her from a court appearance last year. Sutton and Durant then park their car outside the office of Honey West & Company, and Durant lectures, "That is who you have been playing footsie with." He strongly advises him to drop the attempt and find another bank. Sutton, noting the amount of loot at risk, refuses. "When it's over what are you going to do with her?" Durant inquires. "Kill her, what else?" Sutton snarls.

Back at the office, Mr. Tweedy paces and mentions hearing from the home office that Acme Security is perplexed how their systems were so easily compromised. "The man who installed them—Durant—is supposed to be absolutely one of the best...." Sam suddenly deduces that since Durant wired the banks, he could just as easily bypass them. He also realizes that Durant must have recognized Honey from her previous court appearance. He is worried that she has not checked in as scheduled, but Honey suddenly calls and he begins grilling her. Sutton then cuts in and instructs him to get into his truck and await instructions. He complies and is struck from behind. Meanwhile, Sutton and his gang are cutting through the bank wall and placing explosive charges. Honey, completely bound, watches helplessly. Sam, meanwhile, manages to turn the tables on his captor and drives off to the bank as Sutton blows the door open and absconds with both the money and Honey. Sam arrives at the scene after they departed, then remembers that manhole cover in the alleyway. He and the lieutenant race over to it, lift the cover and apprehend one of Sutton's men hiding there. After some friendly persuasion, the hood leads them to Sutton's hiding place, an old ice house. Sam and the lieutenant charge in and a gunfight erupts while Honey remains off to the side, totally bound. The hoods are all subdued, with Sutton crashing down in a pile of ice cubes. "How about that?" Sam asks. "Sutton on the rocks!" "You've got to admit, Sam," Honey intones, "when I cool it, I really cool it." Back at the office, a shivering Honey is trying to get warm. Mr. Tweedy then enters and Sam presents her with his check for good services. Tweedy then lifts his ice-laden drink in her face and offers a toast, to which Honey exclaims, "Hip, hip hooray, Mr. Tweedy!"– and staggers off to keep warm.

"How Brillig O, Beamish Boy"

(Aired January 7, 1966)

Starring: John McGiver (Mr. Brillig), Norman Alden (Ben Fancher), Howard Dayton (Little Ardo), Monte Hale (Sheriff Johnson), Leon Lontoc (Wong), Charles Horvath (Terk).

Script: Don Ingalls

Directed by: Ida Lupino

Sam Bolt walks out of the Bank of Commerce and is immediately tailed by mysterious strangers. Sensing he is being followed, Sam passes an envelope to Honey West, waiting in her car, and she roars off. Sam then ducks into an alley, turns his jacket inside out, and puts on a hat and glasses. After the two strangers run past him, Sam re-emerges onto the street, where a blind man asks him for assistance. He cordially complies and turns to leave, at which point the "blind" man clouts him with his cane. He then signals for the two other thugs to help, and Sam's limp body is carried off, leaving behind only his hat and glasses. Back at the office, Honey paces anxiously back and forth. "Quit worrying, Honey, good guys never die young," Aunt Meg reassures her. "You're misquoting," Honey blurts and the calls Ben Fancher, their client, whose envelope they were entrusted with. The hotel informs her that he checked out without leaving a forwarding address. Honey then tears open the envelope and discovers half a million dollars in large bills. She is about to call the police when, suddenly, the door bell rings. Honey tells Aunt Meg to stash the money somewhere while she answers the door. Honey enters the office to discover Mr. Brillig, a dapper and eloquent gentlemen, who hands her a bouquet of flowers. Brillig is there to propose a trade. "Mr. Brillig, what are we talking about?" she inquires. "Ahhh… impetuous youth–straight to the point," he intones. Specifically, he wants to swap Fancher's package for Sam–before something bad happens to him. "How unfortunate for him if you refuse my kind offer to trade," Brillig declares. When Honey angrily demands that he leave, the door opens again and Brillig's two accomplices step inside. He gives her two hours to make the trade then steps back. The two thugs suddenly pull their guns and Honey declares, "Down, boys–you do have them over-trained!" Before departing, Honey slips Brillig a pair of glasses, actually a radio transmitter, and says that Sam can hardly see a thing without them. "Ahhh, … the female mystique! Such concern. Such tenderness. Such regard for everything–except his life," he notes.

The phone rings again, only this time it's Ben Fancher. He instructs Honey to bring the package to Wong's Curio Shop on 5th Street and she complies. "Woman's work," she blurts and darts out the door. At Wong's she informs Fancher that there will be no trade without Sam being released unharmed. Fancher declares her missing partner is not his problem and she angrily remonstrates, "Well, it better be if you ever expect to get that package back!" Wong steps up and suggests purchasing a dragon fang lamp for good luck. A shot suddenly rings out, smashes the lamp, and Fancher ducks out the back. "Mister Wong, if I were you I wouldn't try to push any more of those lamps!" she says while darting out the door. The scene cuts to the criminal's room, where Sam is bound up and forced to watch violent TV Westerns due to Brillig's short and insecure henchman. He calls him "Shorty" and the thug put a knife to his throat. Brillig then enters, dresses down his psychotic accomplice and gives Sam his "glasses." The two then depart for lunch, whereupon Sam works his hands free and hooks his glasses up to the TV set.

The crooks return soon after and Brillig notices that Sam's

glasses are gone. One thug discovers that Sam's glasses have been electronically tied to the television as a power source. "Well, my boy, we shall use your little scheme for our own purposes," Brillig gloats. "We will prepare a trap to catch some honey!" Sure enough, Honey traces the signal to the apartment and opens the door, while Sam, bound and gagged, tries to warn her off. "Well, if it isn't Malice in wonderland," she blurts while being captured. Once "Little Otto" is engrossed by a war film, Honey motions for Sam to kick him as he adjusts the TV. Sam does so with a resounding thump, spraining his foot in the process, and the two escape. Back at the office, Sam is soaking his injured foot and Honey asks, "Really, Sam, you've just got to stop booting hard heads." "I'll try to kick the habit," is his sorry riposte. Honey walks off in a huff, going "eeewwwwwww!" in faux disgust. Meanwhile, Aunt Meg is busy knitting a chest warmer for Bruce the ocelot when Fancher calls again, instructing Honey to meet him at an abandoned mine. She storms off without Sam and drives down a muddy, ghost town in the rain. Bruce, resplendent in his new chest warmer, remains in the car. The two meet at the mine entrance and immediately come under gunfire from Brillig and his goons, who chase them into the shaft. "They're going to kills us!" Fancher declares and Honey insists that, "If that's the case, would you mind telling me what I am dying for?" Fancher explains that he and Brillig ran a gambling syndicate and that he stole their operating funds and placed them in a security box. A year later Brillig remains unrelenting in his pursuit. As the hoods approach, Honey uses a flare to drive them back temporarily, for neither has a gun. They once again close in for the kill, so Honey orders Fancher to push an old coal cart down the tracks and she drives them back again. Honey finally corners Brillig as Sam and a sheriff arrive to apprehend them. Sam mentions that they will need the half million dollars as evidence, and Honey pulls back Bruce's chest warmer, revealing where it was stashed all along. "Honey, all that money on him–he could have heard the call of the wild and taken off!" he protests. "Yeah," Honey notes, "and with nine lives he would have had a ball!"

"King of the Mountain"

(Aired January 14, 1966)

Starring: David Opatoshu (Kelso King), Dennis Patrick (Carson), Charles Lane (Mr. Ash), Richard Kiel (Grolago), Allyson Ames (Ida Berring), Troy Melton (guard).

Script: Jay Simms

Directed by: Thomas Carr

Shots are fired in an expensive house as a shadowy figure–Sam Bolt–crashes through the window and scampers over to Honey West's car. He was photographing the tax returns of a wealthy suspect when the owner suddenly entered and pulled a gun. As their car roars off, Honey notes that the one remaining suspect on their list, Ida Berring, is a nurse and something of a swinger. "She has a playpen out on Highland Avenue," Sam notes. "Let's shake it and see if it rattles," Honey replies. However, the two arrive outside Berring's place just as she is being murdered. The next day Sam and Honey appear at a board meeting hosted by Mr. Ash, company chairman, and they explain that Sam broke into his house the previous evening and photographed his tax records. Honey reminds Ash that they were hired to check out all company personnel. "Last night was your turn on the barrel," Sam assures him. "You're clean like the rest of them." Discussion next turns to the deceased Ida Berring, the personal nurse of tycoon Kelso King, company owner. "Obviously, she knew more than a good nurse should," Honey interjects. The reclusive King is the object of Ash's interest for he has not been seen for eight years and rumors about his health are driving the company's stock down. "And he gets rich that way?" Honey asks. "I'd like to meet him!" Ash beams while informing Honey that he has already arranged for her to be interviewed as King's replacement nurse that afternoon. Back at their office, Honey is outfitted with Sam's latest array of gadgets, including a wrist camera, a microphone thermometer, and a transceiver in her handbag. "A bugged bag," she notes. "Bully!" They learn from King's dossier that he withdrew from society after being shot in the shoulder by a disgruntled investor, wounds which left him unable to control his own body temperature. "King can't control his body heat–but who can?" Sam jibes her. "Watch your voltage, Sam!" she mockingly exclaims.

Honey motors up to the isolated mansion of Mr. King, while Sam, posing as a telephone repairman, watches nervously from outside. King's secretary, Mr. Carlson, is impressed by "Mrs. Miller's" credentials and will show them to King. He especially appreciates her sense of humor. "You ought to catch my act in surgery," Honey says with a smile. "You left them in stitches?" Carlson retorts. Honey begins snooping around and her hand accidentally triggers a hidden door from which Grolago, a huge and frightening assistant, stands behind. He orders her to sit down and Honey is introduced to King–a humorless, stern figure, who hands her the list of medication she is to prepare–he will administer them himself. Honey manages to place the microphone/thermometer in a potted plant and departs for the kitchen. Honey cautiously resumes snooping around, while hulking Grolago is instructed to spy on her. He nearly catches her but Honey rushes into the kitchen pretending to make the tea. Later she contacts Sam by microphone and instructs him to meet her by the fence that evening.

The two rendezvous in Sam's van and develop the photos taken of Mr. King. Honey immediately notes the man has no shoulder scar and deduces he must be a fake. "It's a ringer, but why?" Sam ponders. "Whatever happened to Kelso King, the answer is in that house," she insists. Honey steals back into the house, observed by Grolago. An angry Carlson calls the main gate and has them trace Mrs. Miller's license plates. Sam, listening in, hears that they are headed to Honey's room and alerts her. "They're on the way to your room right now, get out of there!" he yells. Grolago suddenly kicks the door open, and Honey trips him and escapes. Carlson is subsequently informed that "Mrs. Miller" is a private detective, slams the phone down and discovers the microphone Honey planted in the flower vase. He orders King to turn up the hi-fi to drown it out. Meanwhile, Honey is engaged in a frantic cat-and-mouse chase with Grolago–she is on the point of escaping until inadvertently locking herself in the closet. "Take me to your leader," Honey whimpers when finally cornered. She is hauled before an angry Carlson, who admits he has the real Kelso King under wraps and will dispose of him shortly in an "airplane accident" to drive the company stocks down. The fake King will then make his appearance, deny his death, and company stock will rise–with Carson firmly in control. Honey then feigns amnesia when asked where Sam is. "Where is he? Where is he?" she smiles and keeps repeating. Sam, meanwhile, breaks into the house and looks for her. Carson is getting ready to dip Honey into the hot spring located in the cellar, but she escapes and collides headlong into Sam. "Hey, if the date's off, give me back my fraternity pin!" she jests. The two duck into the cellar with Grolago in hot pursuit, and they dispose of him after a stiff fight. They are then hailed by the real Kelso King, kept behind bars in his own basement. After tossing electric wires into the hot spring, they manage to lure Carson and King's impersonator into their grasp. "Hello, Mr. Carson!" she taunts them. The two criminals fall into the spring and are subdued. Honey begins hovering over the real Kelso King, whom she genuinely likes, and Sam protests. She insists that she did call another nurse for him, yet he demands to know her name. "What's her name? What's her name?" Honey continues blurting, stalling for time.

"It's Earlier Than You Think"

(Aired January 21, 1965)

Starring: James Griffith (Conrad Wicherly No. 1), Leonid Kinskey (Conrad Wicherly No. 2), Maurice Dallimore (Hurd), Bill McLean (Pringle), Bill Catching (Paul Wicherly), Ken Lynch (Lieut. Barney), Paul Sorensen (Patrolman Cowan).

Script: Marc Brandel

Directed by: James Brown

Shots are fired in an expensive house as a Lincolnesque-figure crashes through the window and onto the street. "Fakes! Cheats! Liars!" he exclaims before mounting a horse and galloping down the street. He then he espies the office of H. West & Company, ties his horse to the fence, and stumbles into Honey's office muttering something about Lincoln's assassination. "Box Number 3," he gasps. "No, no, it's wrong ...We've got to stop it!" He then hands her an authentic-looking newspaper dated April 15, 1865, whereby the president's murder is announced, and dies. "I hate to lose the most interesting client we've ever had," Honey intones. "You've already lost him!" Aunt Meg interjects. Honey and Aunt Meg decide to hide the body before calling the police, but an officer enters the room demanding to know whose horse is parked outside. The scene switches to police headquarters where Sam and Honey explain what they know to an irate Lieutenant Barney, who explains that the victim was Paul Wicherly, an eccentric collector as well as an authority on Abraham Lincoln. His only living relative is his brother, the equally eccentric Conrad Wicherly. The duo then depart–without mentioning the newspaper– and drive separate ways until Honey is accosted at the corner by a man in highland garb, claiming to be Conrad Wicherly, the deceased man's brother. Honey gives him a lift to his hotel, asking, "Shall we take the high road or the low road?" while denying any knowledge of the newspaper he is seeking. No sooner does Honey depart than she is hailed by a second man posing as Conrad Wicherly, who inquires if his dead brother gave her a newspaper. Again she denies any knowledge and drops him off at his hotel. Back at their office, Sam and Honey encounter a third man posing as Conrad Wicherly, a soft-spoken Southerner with a distinct drawl, who inquires about a newspaper, a *Washington Star* of April 15, 1865. This individual does not drive, and has no identification–but he does produce a cashier's check for $500,000–he was going to buy his brother's collection. Sam and Honey deny any knowledge of the paper and he departs.

Her interest peaked, Honey sends Sam off to get a Photostat copy of the real *Washington Star* of that date. She then goes to Mr. Pringle, a scientist friend, who explains the process of radioactive Carbon 14 dating to her. Somewhat perplexed by the explanation, he assures her that the paper in question is real. Honey asks if the process can be faked. "Not unless somebody has discovered a way of radioactively aging matter–and nobody has," he insists. Realizing that she is carrying a "hot" item, Honey mails the newspaper off to herself and leaves the building. Suddenly, she is kidnapped by both Conrad Wicherlys. "Hello, I didn't recognize you at first without your kilt," she mocks her captor. "Shut up," is his brusque response. Honey keeps talking–having turned on her necklace microphone—and Sam, listening in, discerns she is being held at Maple Heights–at the house with a "For Sale" sign in front. The two crooks tie Honey up and threaten to expose her to their radioactive aging machine. "It changes the isotope of Carbon 14," she informs her incredulous captors. "Everybody's talking about isotopes these days," she explains. The two intend to turn it on her face if she does not tell them where the newspaper is. Thinking quick, Honey informs Conrad Witcherly No. 1 that his accomplice, named Roger, was also posing as the deceased victim. The two men begin arguing as to whom was about to blackmail who–while Honey begins sawing through her ropes with a sharp ring. As the two fight, Honey frees herself and points the aging machine to back them off. Roger manages to pull the plug but she flees upstairs to a waiting Sam. The two return to the cellar but the crooks have escaped.

By now Honey realizes that Paul Wicherly recognized something phony about the newspaper when the two men tried to sell it to him. "Well, you've got the paper–we're in good shape," Sam concludes. Honey disagrees, insisting, "But they know that I know that they know that I know. They're going try to close that deal with Paul Wicherly right away!" The two crooks are indeed trying to sell a forged collection of Abraham Lincoln's love letters to Wicherly, but he wishes he could see the newspaper that they were wrapped in. The two men assure him of the collection's authenticity, at which point he hands them a half-million dollars. Suddenly, Honey and Sam suddenly barge through the door. She shows Witcherly a copy of the real *Washington Star*, which states that the president was sitting in Box Number Eight when he was killed, and not Number Three–that's why his brother knew it was a forgery. The crooks pull out their guns then make off with the cash, but Sam and Honey drop them in the corridor just as a policeman shows up in the elevator. That evening Sam, Honey and Meg are all set for a night on the town when Meg, marveling over menus printed in the newspapers, states that a three-course meal costs only 23 cents. "At those prices I'll take you both to dinner," Sam replies. But who should appear at the door but the same cop who asks, "All right–now what are you going to do with this horse?"

"The Perfect Un-Crime"

(Aired January 28, 1966)

Starring: David Brian (Mr. Rockwell), John Harmon (engineer), Bryon Foulger (Arthur Bird), James Secrest (stock boy), Bob Stephenson (watchman).

Script: Ken Kolb

Directed by: Sidney Miller

Sam Bolt and Honey West are lurking in a darkened alley when they perceive what looks like a gun barrel sticking around a corner. Sam charges to disarm the handler, only to charge headlong into a local drunk and his wine bottle. The duo apologize and continue looking for clues left by a mysterious client they are supposed to meet. Sam declares his misgivings about arranging the rendezvous by telephone, but Honey insists, "No, he had an honest voice." "And you'd know an honest voice?" he asks. Continuing leads guide them up a fire escape, into a darkened room, where somebody grabs Sam. A struggle ensues before Honey turns on the light to reveal Sam wrestling their client, Arthur Bird, to the ground. Bird, a very modest, nondescript figure, explains his remarkable predicament. Bird is chief clerk in accounting at a large department store and he emotes about all the money that passes through his hands daily. "Hold it,"

Honey interjects. "Are you asking us to help you rob that store?" "Oh, no, no, no!" Bird protests, opening a suitcase full of money, "I already did that—I want to hire you to put it back!" Honey immediately accepts the challenge, much to Sam's utter disbelief. "We'd have to perform a burglary in reverse," he exclaims. "That's the part that appeals to me," Honey counters. "We'd be the first to ever un-rob a safe!" Bird describes carefully how he began playing a harmless little game about stealing the money and living with native girls on Bora Bora–then changed his mind when he learned that they only speak French. He is also smitten by a guilty conscience. "I found out that I'm honest," he whimpers. "There, there," Honey consoles him. "It could have happened to anybody!"

Their plot to help Mr. Bird unfolds the next day as a haughty Aunt Meg shows up at the office of Mr. Rockwell, the store manager, to exchange a pair of pajamas. As he convinces her to go downstairs for a refund, she carefully makes observations as to the room's layout and where the safe is. "Why do you have locks on the windows?" she inquires. "To keep me from jumping out on days like this," Rockwell fires back. Back at the office, Meg explains what she saw and informs Honey that she also chatted with Mr. Bird in accounting. Honey rules out entering through the windows, which are always closed, and decides upon a routine break-in followed by disarming the alarm system. That afternoon commotion breaks out in the store as Honey "accidentally" gets her umbrella stuck in the elevator. Sam, disguised as an electrician, next comes in and, when nobody is looking, shuts off the alarm and absconds with the freight elevator access keys. The two meet in the van, parked outside, and grow apprehensive when Mr. Bird shows up late. He has been badly beaten by people looking for the money and now cannot accompany them into the building. Worse, the trio is also stuck with the money that has to be accounted for on the morrow. "We may all have to learn French," Sam indignantly notes. "Don't be ridiculous," Honey protests. "What's a girl to do on Bora Bora?" Sam shoots a look of disbelief, then smiles. Bird subsequently gives them the vault combination and they drop him off at their office to convalesce. "I hope I gave them the right combination to the safe," Bird confesses to Meg, "I was so groggy I'm afraid I got it all wrong!"

Returning to the store, Sam and Honey have no difficulty breaking in and disposing of the night watchman with chloroform, and then make their way to the manager's office. After fumbling with the safe–Bird gave them the wrong combination–Sam reverses the first two numbers and manages to break it open. "What a job! Rounding third and heading for home!" he exults. The duo are in the act of replacing the money stole when the lights suddenly go on and the duo are confronting the manager and his assistant–guns drawn. "Thrown out at the plate...," Honey muses. It turns out that Rockwell was onto Bird's little game all along and intends to acquire all the money he stole. Sam and Honey are forced to put the money back in the bag and hand it over to them. "Don't you see, Sam? He's going to keep the money and let Arthur go to jail," she deduces. At a given signal Honey suddenly knocks the guns from their hands with her cape and the two bolt down the hallway, suitcase in hand. A madcap chase ensues through various store departments as Rockwell and his assistant track them down in the dark, without success. In the middle of the hunt, the groggy night watchman awakens and calls the police. Honey and Sam continue dodging their pursuers and finally disable them with billiard balls just as police sirens begin wailing. "We'll never get this money back in the safe," Sam exclaims. "I've got a better idea," Honey shoots back. "Let's leave them holding the bag!" The two flee just ahead of the cops. The next day Mr. Bird arrives at their office to sincerely express his gratitude. "I am so happy to go to work," he declares. "Just think, if things had gone wrong I'd been in Bora Bora this morning with some native girl." Sam then asks where Honey is going in the middle of the work day. It turns out she glimpsed an attractive dress during last night's chase through the women's department and—considering what she just endured—Honey is determined to buy it!

"Like Visions and Omens... and All That Jazz"

(Aired February 4, 1966)

Starring: Nehemiah Persoff (Faustini), Fred Beir (Peter Lynch), Norman Alden (Arty Dickson), June Vincent (Vicky Tillson), Mimsy Farmer (Tina), Benny Rubin (Marty).

Script: Tony Barrett

Directed by: John Florea

A Cessna airplane pulls up to an aircraft hanger as Tina Tillson, a wealthy socialite's daughter, climbs aboard. Peter Lynch, the pilot, urges her to sky dive with safety. She jumps and Vicky Tillson, her mother, watches in anguish as Tina cannot open her chute-but manages pull the cord at the last minute. Watching this drama unfold are Sam and Honey, parked at the end of the runway. They have been hired by Mrs. Tillson to find out who is trying to murder her daughter. They rush up to Tina, who is shaken but unharmed and says, "You were right. I have a reason to be scared. Real scared." That evening Lynch is playing with his jazz trio at The Gilded Cage, a swank nightclub, with Sam and Honey in the corner, watching his every move. Who should walk in but Tina, who takes a seat and begins making eyes at Peter. Meanwhile, Mrs. Tillson consults with fortune teller Faustini, who has correctly predicted a host of near-fatal accidents plaguing her daughter. "Oh, cosmos! Oh, universe!" he emotes, "Why? Why such trouble and darkness for one so young!" Sam, listening from the truck, murmurs, "Boy... ham on rye ..." Back at the office, Honey dresses down Mrs. Tillson for not informing her about Faustini, who she suspects is somehow connected Tina's rash of near-tragedies - all of which he uncannily predicted. Tillson declares that she usually hires him to entertain at parties and, moreover, he has never been near Tina. "Maybe he's doing a little more than just predicting," Honey skeptically notes. To get more information on Faustini, Honey drops by her friend Marty, a talent agent, who dismisses Faustini as a run-down actor who found his niche as a "predictor." She asks him how he operates, and Mary says he has an insider check out all his clients for background information. As she leaves Honey also observes Marty's newest act, three muscle men posing to classical music. "Let them grow their hair and get them guitars," she says. "They can't miss!"

Back at the Gilded Cage, Peter and Tina depart for the evening. She crosses the street as, suddenly, a dark sedan races right for her. Sam, watching from across the street, pushes her out of harm's way. Honey gets the license plate and traces the vehicle back to Arty Dickson, one of Tina's former flames. She pays a call on Dickson, a bookie and sleazy womanizer who calls Honey "Chicky." He plays coy—until she flips him over her shoulder. Arty finally confesses that he was paid $200 to run his car at Mrs. Tillson-although he has no idea who hired or paid him. "No sentiment, Arty?" Honey intones. "Last year's romance?" "Sentiment?" he asks. "What has romance got to do with business?!" Back in the van, Sam and Honey run down the facts, all centered upon Faustini's ability to set up - then predict - near-tragedies. Honey considers him, "A phony predictor who calls the shots and makes sure they happen on schedule." After all, the rash of accidents was most likely designed to simply terrorize Tina, not kill her. She deduces that some kind of big payoff is in the offing-and soon. Meanwhile, Tina gets a phone call from Arty, who urges her to come by his place immediately-but will not say why. Eager to see an old friend, she shows up and finds that Arty has been killed. A shadowy figure suddenly grabs and chloroforms her, then rubs her fingerprints on the murder weapon.

Sam and Honey argue over Arty's murder, the lack of a murder weapon, Tina's disappearance, and what it all means. She sends him off to try to find Tina, while Honey intends to check out what the cosmos will reveal. "Faustini?" Sam inquires. "Good prediction!" she replies. Honey steals into Faustini's darkened mansion and begins rifling through his drawers and papers. The light suddenly goes on and he is standing there, gun drawn. "Miss West, I predict a very unhappy future for you!" he states. Honey smiles at him, noting that he simply does the predicting – murder is not his style. "When's the pay off?" she asks. "Tonight? How much?" Suddenly, a darkened figure leans into the window and shoots Faustini dead. Honey then races over to Mrs. Tillson's posh house, where she is preparing a large suitcase full of money to buy the weapon that killed Arty Dickson. This is the payoff: blackmail. Honey decides to take the money to Peter herself, whom she believes was behind the entire scheme from its onset. Sam contacts her by microphone, begging Honey not to go further. "I want you out of this! He's killed two men!" he screams. "Sam, don't talk and drive at the same time–it's dangerous," she responds. Honey takes the money to a hangar and is accosted at gunpoint by Peter, who motions to take her skydiving–*sans* parachute. Fortunately, Sam pulls up just as they head to the plane and Honey escapes. Peter then revs up his craft and chases Sam around the field while Honey runs over to a forklift. Peter deplanes and dashes back to the hangar where Honey chases and catches him, lifting the crook overhead. Sam races up and grins, stating, "Main floor, last stop!" as she lowers him to ground level. Back at the Gilded Cage, Sam and Honey are enjoying a night out, serenaded by a new jazz band, and marveling over the large check Mrs. Tillson has generously provided for their services. Suddenly, the acts change when the Sophisticates–the three long-haired musclemen–arrive on stage playing guitars. "Oh, no....I wonder who ever dreamed up that act," Sam ponders in disgust. "You wouldn't believe it, Sam!" Honey declares.

"Don't Look Now, But Isn't That Me?"

(Aired February 11, 1965)

Starring: Alan Reed (Chick), Louis Quinn (Toddle), Monica Keating (Mrs. Carter), Jonathan Hole (Mr. Gruder), Charles Horvath (Ding Dong), Paul Sorensen (police officer), Anne Francis (Pandora Fox).

Script: Gwen Bagni, Paul Dubov

Directed by: James Brown

At a posh social gathering, Honey West steps out and is lauded by Mrs. Carter, who has hired her to guard her guest's expensive fur coats. Many of the male guests look on approvingly and longingly. "Honey" actually turns out to be Pandora Fox, a dead ringer for Honey and part of a ring of professional thieves. She lets her gang into the store room and they make off with all the valuable items. The door bell then rings and the real Honey West, escorted by Sam Bolt, makes her entrance. This comes much to the surprise of the owner, who expresses amazement that Honey managed to alter her attire so quickly. "Now didn't you stir quite enough attention tonight without changing your gown in the middle of the evening?" she asks with a smile. Honey and Sam immediately suspect the worst and, running up to the safe room, discover the fur coats missing. "Don't look now, Sam, but I think somebody else is me...," Honey declares.

Back at the office, the duo begins running through how the crooks would know that they were hired to protect the furs. Sure enough, Sam finds a bug attached to the phone. However, Honey insists that the device not be unplugged. "Relax, Sam, we're just turning a wire *tap* into a wire *trap*," she insists. The thieves, meanwhile, are busy studying film footage of Honey to better mimic her every move. However, Chick, the boss, is having trouble motivating Pandora to take her work more seriously. She protests her treatment in a thick Brooklyn accent, declaring, "Listen to who's talkin' here–Mister Poi-fect!" Chick especially recoils at her pronunciation of "fine"–which comes out "foy–ine," and insists that she work on it. Suddenly, one crook alerts the others that Honey's office is receiving a call. Actually, the caller is Aunt Meg impersonating Amelia Pruett, a rich woman soliciting a female detective to guard her rich jewels, valued at $300,000. Honey "agrees" to meet her outside the bank at 10:15 AM. "Did you hear that?" Chick sarcastically asks Pandora. "Foy-ine!" she replies.

The next day, Aunt Meg, bedecked in a fur coats and a feather hat, waits outside the bank for Honey to rendezvous as planned. Sam is nearby in the van, observing Pandora as she waits outside the bank. However, as Honey pulls up and attempts to park nearby, one of the crooks feigns being hit by her car. As he lies on the ground howling in pain, a policeman shows up and suddenly he is all right. "Oh, no, not you again, Miss West!" he bemoans. Honey insists that the accident is fake, yet the cop insists on seeing her license and during their argument the perpetrator escapes. "That's a switch," Honey intones, "a hit and run pedestrian." Simultaneously, Ding Dong, a large and none-to bright hood, enters the van and holds Sam hostage. Aunt Meg then runs into Pandora, who feigns laryngitis, and takes the jewels. However, Meg notices the hood in Sam's van and tries to stall for time. She wrestles with "Honey" and accidentally rips off her blonde coiffure. Her brunette locks exposed, Pandora exclaims, "Yikes!" and runs off with the jewels. Sam, meanwhile, disposes of Ding Dong with a single punch as Honey pulls up. Meg proudly brandishes her trophy, declaring, "Well, talk about flipping your wig!"

Back at the office, Sam and Honey are profusely apologizing to each other for blowing the assignment–much to Aunt Meg's amazement. Honey suddenly realizes that the wig Meg grabbed is their best clue. She follows up by visiting the maker and asking for a duplicate wig–then inquires if he still has her address. "I'll never understand women," he confesses. "Blondes want to be brunettes and brunettes want to be blondes!" He obliging shows a picture of her with the address on it and she reads off "1128 Crystal, Apartment 22 – that's right." Honey and Sam park the van outside the address when a car pulls up, Pandora steps out and Chick instructs her to stay put until he is ready to move. Sam wants to pick her up immediately, but Honey stops her, noting, "Girl talk!" She knocks on the door, Pandora gasps in horror, and is pushed aside. Gazing upon her perfect double, Honey says, "I've heard of being two-faced but this is ridiculous!" Pandora tries to escape and Honey flips her to the floor, then contacts her partner. "You can come up now, Sam," she declares. "You're missing the double feature!" Sam takes Pandora to the office for safe keeping, while Honey squeezes into one of Pandora's ultra-tight dresses. Suddenly, one of the crooks enters the room and Honey – this time impersonating her impersonator – plays coy with him before knocking him out. Soon after Chick and Ding Dong appear and she slips out with them. Chick soon catches on that Pandora is fake, so he takes her to the house of a magician friend where the stolen furs are kept behind a hidden door. The trio begins unloading the furs when Chick finally exposes Honey's act and pulls a gun. "You made two mistakes, Miss West. That beauty mark, very attractive, but Pandora doesn't have one. Also she can't say *fine*," he growls. Sam suddenly appears and tears into Ding Dong while Honey spars with Chick. They prevail after a good brawl and Sam inquires, "Are you all right?" Foy-ine! Just foy-ine!" Honey says. They return to the office to deal with Pandora and ask Aunt Meg where she is. They find the tough-talking moll curled up on a chair, sneezing like crazy and cowering from the ocelot. "Poor girl," Aunt Meg declares. "She's allergic to Bruce!"

"Come to Me, My Litigation Baby"

(Aired February 11, 1965)

Starring: Ellen Corby (Nellie Peedy), James Brown (Buster Macon), Michael Fox (Mr. Strate), Army Archerd, Chuck Couch (Witness No. 1), Bill Shannon (Witness No. 2), Ron Lerner (Dancer No. 1), Kami Stevens (Dancer No. 2).

Script: Gwen Bagni, Paul Dubov

Directed by: Thomas Carr

Sam and Honey have been hired by an insurance company to investigate what they feel might be a phony accident claim. The main suspect is Nellie Peedy, an elderly old lady, who is pushing Buster Macon, the wheelchair-bound suspect, to the movies. "If that little old lady wheels him into the court room the jury is going to beg him to take the money" she muses. "You're a born cynic," Sam retorts. The duo continues observing from their parked van and suddenly, Honey notices that Peedy is ducking behind the theater and enters Leo's Gym so she elects to follow. Once inside, Honey is immediately accosted by the muscular door guard, who does not allow women. When she insists that Mrs. Peedy just entered, he gets physical with Honey and she chops him down. Honey then darts into the gym room and calls for Peedy without luck. The attendant insists she leave at once and a disbelieving Honey reluctantly complies. Old Mrs. Peedy, however, was up on a lift, and she jumps down onto the trampoline, does an expert flip, and lands on the floor. Back in the van, Sam and Honey argue over the necessity of watching what is very likely nothing when they notice that the muscular attendant goes into the theater and pushes Macon along in his wheelchair. Back at their office, Honey confers with Mr. Strate, the insurance representative, as to the upcoming lawsuit–and a possible $300,000 payout. His company is willing to pay off any legitimate claim, but they feel that Macon's claim that he tripped over torn carpet in a very posh hotel simply strains credulity. Honey agrees and requests a sample of the torn carpet for analysis. Meanwhile, Mrs. Peedy is walking down the street and deliberately walks into an expensive Rolls-Royce, faking both an injury and intense pain. A bystander walks over and offers his services as an eyewitness. Sam watches the entire set-up and informs Honey by phone. "Sam, you're so gracious, are you trying to tell me I'm right?" she chides him. At the time, Honey is also tailing the gym attendant, who is visiting a very expensive hotel. Sure enough, he drops a banana on the ground and trips on it, faking serious injuries–when another bystander steps up and offers his services as a witness.

Sam and Honey deduce they are onto a slick accident ring. She then spots Macon from the van, wheeling himself to a magazine stand, and Honey decides to go out and get acquainted. Honey easily catches his eye with her good looks and phony Southern accent, and he convinces her to allow him to carry her bags. Sam steps up, disguised as a street photographer, and offers to take her picture. Macon angrily waves him off, then Honey drops her bag of oranges and pretends to slip–and Macon miraculously stands to catch her. Sam then runs over to photograph him, trips on the oranges, and snaps a photo of the sky. Back at the office, Honey continues analyzing the carpet sample and she concludes it was cut. Sam questions its validity in court. Honey, however has nagging suspicion that frail, old Mrs. Peedy is somehow connected and that Leo's Gym is actually the center of things. "Lady wrestlers go to gyms," she notes, "petite Peedys do not. Let's take a look, Sam." She and Sam stake the gym out late at night and observe the attendant open up, and he is joined by the men who had witnessed both fake accidents. "Hail, hail, the gang's all here," Sam intones. "Altogether it spells fraud."

Sam and Honey next arrange a fake fire to bug Buster's phone and they go to his apartment complex. While he watches television, Sam tosses a smoke bomb into his room and he wheels himself in the corridor, where Honey stands with a camera. Her cover blown, Macon berates her while Sam enters the room from outside and plants the bug. They next hear Buster calling the gym, saying they have a "blonde problem" and that he's coming over. Sam and Honey decide likewise to hit the gym, where they take a perch in the rafters. Both watch in amazement as frail Mrs. Peedy is teaching her underlings how to stage fake car accidents, replete with fake screaming and agony. "I see it but I can't believe it," Honey whispers. "Me Tarzan...you Jane," Sam whispers back, pointing to training ropes hanging nearby. They both swing down upon the culprits and engage them in a terrific brawl. Honey calls upon Mrs. Peedy to surrender and she snarls, "I warn you, I don't play fair!" Peedy then tosses several juggling pins at Honey, who has to duck, and the rowdies are gradually subdued. Who should walk in but Buster Macon, who lunges at Honey, then trips over the juggling pins she tosses at him. "Glad to see you all up and around again!" she sneers. Honey then looks around for Peedy, finding her high above them on a trapeze swing. "Mrs. Peedy, would you come down here, please?" she asks. Mrs. Peedy complies by dropping on the trampoline, does an expert flip, and lands on the floor. Taken aback, Honey says, "Sam, isn't it wonderful to grow old gracefully?" That evening Sam entertains Honey at a discotheque, where the local emcee introduces a special dance called "The Honey West Walk." Enticed by the jazzy rock score, Honey convinces Sam to get up and dance, at which point he falls over. Honey then leaps on him, declaring, "It was a beautiful accident, Sir, I saw everything— I'll be your witness!"

"Slay, Gypsy, Slay"

(Aired February 25, 1966)

Starring: Michael Pate (Darza), Putzi (Michael Manza), Byron Morrow (Franklyn Buckley), Arline Anderson (Mrs. Buckley), Papita Funez (Lida), Bobby Johnson (attendant), Jack Perkins (Szabo).

Script: Tony Barrett

Directed by: James Brown

One evening, Honey and Sam are on assignment outside the expensive home of Franklyn Buckley, where a social gathering is unfolding. Sam gets on his radio and grouses over having to wait for nothing and Honey chides him, "Once a job has first begun, never quit until the party's over." Mrs. Buckley then walks out and confesses to Honey that she cannot relax due to threatening phone calls placed to her husband. Suddenly, Sam is knocked out from behind while two large men grab Mr. Buckley, and drag him off to a waiting helicopter. Honey charges over intending to free him and is knocked aside, but not before grabbing an amulet from one of the kidnappers. She then grabs a landing strut and hangs on briefly as the chopper zooms off, but let's go and falls. A groggy Sam runs over screaming, "You planning to go into orbit?" "If only the Wright brothers had left well enough alone!" Honey replies. Back at the office, Honey explains to the police that she has no lead on the kidnapping when Sam calls from the airport and informs her that the helicopter pilot had been held at gunpoint by foreigners and forced to land near Coleville, a desert area south of San Diego. "The last he saw the three of them they were sitting in the sand–just like a low-budget Foreign Legion picture," he notes. Honey then decides to have her "fortune told" and visits a gypsy friend to inquire about the mysterious amulet. Her karate-obsessed contact informs her that it symbolizes the Andaluca gypsy family headed by a man named Darza–a wealthy, dangerous individual who owns property everywhere–including Coleville. The action cuts to outside Coleville, where Sam and Honey are spying on the gypsy camp. He warns her that she simply cannot stroll in the camp. "That's your problem, Sam," Honey declares, holding up gypsy attire. "You just don't think sneaky enough."

Honey, now bedecked with a dark wig and a flowing skirt, is next seen sitting next to Darza, posing as a stranger wandering through the desert. Darza gladly takes her in and, while the rest of the camp sleeps, she begins sneaking around the camp looking for Buckley. As she investigates Darza's wagon, Honey is discovered by Lida, the gypsy dancer. A suspicious Darza asks why and Honey intones, "Full moon...very romantic." He decides to sit with Honey under the moon and lace her with wine to find out more. Suddenly, their reverie is interrupted by a drunken old miner – Sam — who staggers into camp looking for water. Darza hosts him briefly then motions him off. As Honey escorts Sam back to his mule, she whispers, "Talk about over-acting!" Darza slips sleeping pills into Honey's wine. She awakens alone as Sam pulls up in the van to revive her. "Just before dawn I woke up and there were the three wagons 100 yards away–trudging through the desert like the second act in Carmen," he tells her. Sam also mentions that the wagons split up, with Darza heading for the Slender Palm Health Resort. "It's pretty exclusive–they say you need a pedigree to get in there," Honey notes. "That's your problem, Honey - you just don't think sneaky enough," Sam says with a smile–then holds up a skimpy bathing suit for her to wear.

The two blend in easily with the jet-set and Darza, not recognizing Honey, gets reacquainted. She subsequently learns that Darza is not merely a guest at the Slender Palm - he's the owner.

Honey next enters the underground garage and snoops around. She uncovers the missing Franklin Buckley sleeping in a small room, clutching a suitcase stuffed full of money. She slips a small microphone into the suitcase, then departs. Honey and Sam then contacts Mrs. Buckley, who informs them that nearly a million dollars is missing. "Goodbye, kidnapping–hello, embezzlement," Sam declares. Honey concludes that Darza is actually helping Buckley to leave the country somehow. However, Darza and Buckley are actually both onto the investigators and the latter calls and pleads with her to go meet him. Unable to resist the bait, she complies and, while talking to Buckley, Szabo, a large gypsy, hits her from behind and carries her down into the caverns. She revives in front of Darza, who sarcastically informs her, "I think I preferred you as a gypsy." Honey shoots back, "I think I preferred the mickey." The four continue through the caverns, past a cage holding an aggressive gorilla, which Darza explains is there in case certain "customers" need to be reminded who is boss during smuggling operations. Honey is then shown an underground river to Mexico on which Darza conducts his clients to freedom, and where intends to hurl her off. Sam, meanwhile, is closing in, tracing Honey's movements electronically. He attacks just as Honey is about to get tossed and a terrific fight ensues. The duo prevail and chase after Buckley, but not before Darza manages to release the angry gorilla. The ape is unstoppable until Sam grabs a handful of Buckley's security notes, sets them on fire, and chases the gorilla back into his cage. "Oh, you're really the last of the big-time spenders," Honey confesses. Back at the office, Sam presents Honey with two generous checks from Mrs. Buckley and the bank, and a bottle of perfume called "Gypsy Guitars." She then presents him with a gift of her own. "But why a cigarette lighter?" he asks. "The next time a gorilla goes ape I don't want you to have to look for a match!" she muses.

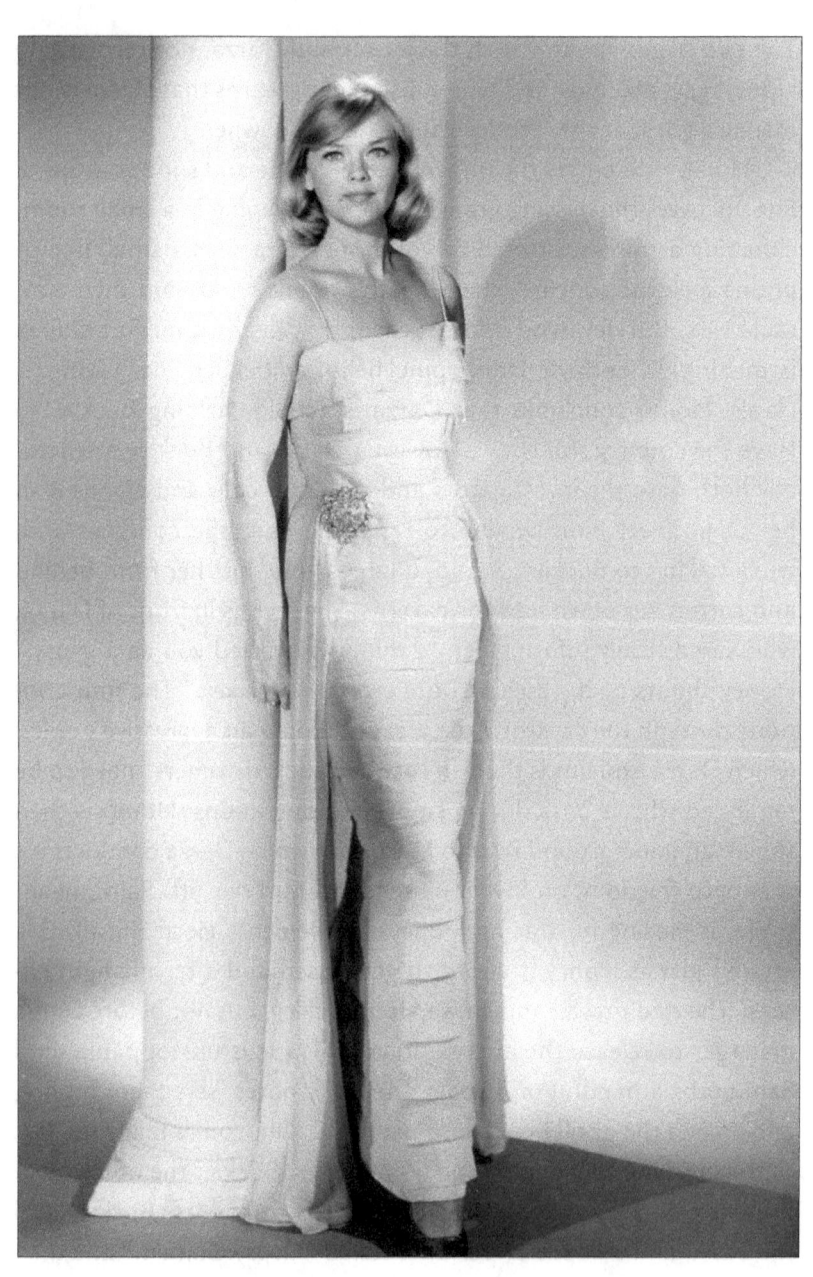

"The Fun-Fun Killer"

(Aired March 4, 1966)

Starring: Marvin Kaplan (Byron Manners), John Hoyt (Professor Von Kemp), Woodrow Parfrey (Ronald Neuworth), William Keene (Granville Manners), Ken Lynch (Lieut. Barney).

Script: Art Weingarten

Directed by: Murray Golden

At night, Granville Manners, an executive with Whiz Bang Toy Company, hurriedly flees from his office and makes for his car. It fails to start, so he runs on foot into the night. The scene cuts to Honey West's office, where she is on the couch with Bruce the ocelot, watching his favorite jungle show. "Bruce," she asks, "why do we always have to watch your show? You see one jungle picture and you've seen them all." Manners then rings the doorbell frantically and Honey lets him in, when he pleads for help. Honey, eager to assist a client, asks why he is so frightened. Suddenly, a mechanical robot crashes through the door and makes for Manners. Honey draws her gun and fires to no effect, and the robot flings her aside. It then closes upon the frightened man. Hours later Lieutenant Barney is in the office saying that the victim was electrocuted by 25,000 volts of electricity. Honey and Sam explain that he was a client and had hired them to check out the management of Fantastic Toys in advance of a possible merger. Barney then asks Honey if the robot had any distinguishing characteristics and she sarcastically replies, "Now that you mention it, he had the cutest little Cary Grant dimple just where his chin ought to be." "Thanks," Barney blurts in disgust, "you're a big help." Once the lieutenant leaves Honey shows Sam a small metal stamping dropped by Manners. When Sam angrily asks why she withheld the evidence from the police they respond in unison, "It's the only clue we have!" The phone then rings and it turns out to be Byron Manners–Mr. Manners nephew–who wants to meet them in a half an hour. "As Sherlock used to say," Honey intones, "'the game's afoot.'"

The two venture to Whiz Bang Toys and encounter Byron Manners, an affable, if toy-obsessed, eccentric who professes no knowledge of why anybody would want to kill his uncle. Honey then asks to see around the factory and Bryon agrees, arranging for his treasurer, Ronald Neuworth, to give her a tour. She also deliberately drops her bag to see if Bryon reacts to the metal stamping, but he hardly notices. Neuworth takes her into the testing laboratory, but gets called away, and she snoops around. Suddenly, she is surprised by Professor Van Kemp, who is in charge of design and testing. Honey then tries to leave, but Neuworth returns and she drops her bag again to check for a reaction. The metal stamping elicits no reaction and she leaves disappointed. Back at the office, Sam informs Honey he was at the Securities and Exchange Commission checking up on Whiz Bang's financial statements. He is suspicious of Byron, who stands to inherit his uncle's share in the company and therefore take control of it. Honey is unconvinced and wants to return to Whiz Bang that evening for another look. Sam is worried about her safety, as usual, and she declares, "Honestly, you'd think this was my first second-story job!" Honey no sooner disappears inside than someone throws Sam a beach ball, which discharges sleeping gas and knocks him out. Meanwhile, she returns to the testing lab and hears noises from behind the closet. Honey connects the noise to the metal stamping she carries, opens the door, and finds the robot there, clicking away. Beating a hasty retreat, she steps outside the office and is promptly tackled by Byron Manners. She flips him over her shoulder, then he confesses to working in his office late when he heard a noise in the lab and went to investigate. "What are *you* doing here?" he demands. Honey takes him back to the closet, opens it, and a dead Professor Van Kemp slumps out. Honey dashes outside, revives Sam, and exclaims that she found the robot—then lost it. Sam groggily demands to know how. "It wasn't easy," she insists. "Somebody traded me a very live robot for a very dead professor!"

Sam and Honey enter the factory and find both the robot – and the dead body – missing. They determine to explore further and Sam quickly finds the robot lurking in the warehouse as it begins tailing him. Honey, poking around the factory section, is also followed by another robot, which she is forced to dodge. "Sam! It must have been mating season—there's another tin woodman here!" she declares. Meanwhile, Sam's robot nearly corners him until he finds a metal stamping attached to his heel-apparently placed there while he was unconscious-and he flings it aside. The robot turns and follows the coin and he dashes off to find Honey. She is having troubles of her own as the robot keeps closing and, when she tosses the coin away, yelling "Go fetch! It's the disc you want, not me!," the robot keeps advancing on her. Desperate, she turns a fan on the automaton and hears the distinct noise of Neuworth coughing from inside the suit. "Your situation is hopeless, Miss West," he insists. "Why not end it quickly?" "I'm the long-suffering type," she counters. Honey then turns a fire extinguisher on the robot, which begins backing off-just as Sam is lowering a huge magnet on him from a ceiling crane. Neuworth is hoisted aloft and apprehended. "How about that," Honey mockingly asks. "They just don't make robots like they used to." Afterwards, Sam explains that Neuworth adamantly opposed the proposed merger because he would lose most of his influence at the company. Von Kemp was killed once he uncovered Neuworth's scheme and was going to expose him. Sam next suggests they go out to dinner, but Honey declines, citing that tonight Bruce has to watch his favorite jungle TV show. Sam slumps down on the couch beside her, muttering, "Oh, brother...."

"Pop Goes the Easel"

(Aired March 11, 1966)

Starring: George Furth, Larry D. Mann (Willis Van Wyck), Anthony Bustrel (Mr. Leopold), Bill Quinn (Lieutenant), Robert Strauss (Barry King), Howard Curtis (the hood), Beau Hickman (waiter).

Script: Teleplay by Lila Garrett and Bernie Kahn; script by Gail Allen and Chris Christensen

Directed by: James Brown

Aunt Meg is shopping for food at a local supermarket and innocently picks out a can of chicken gumbo soup. Suddenly, she is accosted by two men who insist that they turn that particular soup can over to them, but she refuses. "Gentlemen!" she declares. "My chicken gumbo is not on the trading block!" Once out in the parking lost Meg is threatened at knife point for the can of soup, then shoved into a shopping cart and rolled away. Honey West, responding to her screams, rushes over and is nearly knocked down by the thug on his motorcycle as he roars away. Meg, shaken but unhurt, exclaims, "I think we've stumbled onto a ring of cutthroat soup-nappers!" Honey and Sam next visit the art studio of Sandy Corbin, a noted pop artist, who had painted the label of the soup can and placed a foolish bet with his agent, Willis Van Wyck; Corbin wagered that his art was so realistic that it could fool consumers. Sam is astonished–and not a little angry–that Corbin's seemingly realistic artwork commands so much money. Suddenly, Corbin receives a phone call from Barry King, his press agent, and he angrily hangs up on him. "If this is a publicity stunt..," Honey angrily interjects. Sam suggests they take Aunt Meg downtown to identify mug shots. Corbin says there is no need – and produces a life-size cut out of the thief. "That's him!" Meg exclaims. "Look at his face, he's got soup thief written all over him!" Honey decides to take the rendering to various art galleries and see what kind of reaction it stirs. One art dealer, Mr. Leopold, goes crazy over the notion of acquiring a Corbin original and Honey has to fight him off. Meanwhile, Sam visits Barry King, who denies any knowledge of the soup theft. "Publicity stunt?! You flatter me, Mr. Bolt," he says. "You know, if I could pull a stunt like that soup caper, I wouldn't have to be here in this crummy office without a staff and a bunch of screwballs for clients!" Sam stalks out, more convinced than ever that Corbin and King planned the entire episode for publicity. "Come on, let's take this cut-out to the cut-up," Honey angrily declares.

Sam and Honey arrive outside Corbin's studio, and she hauls the life-size cut-out inside. Stumbling about, she trips over a dead body belonging to the soup thief. "Sam, forget about the Corbin copy," she states on her microphone, "we've got the original right here!" Suddenly, someone slugs Honey from behind and Sam runs in to help. He revives her and Honey, looking through the dead man's pockets, retrieves a set of keys to the Hotel Graystone. The duo pays the room a visit and finds the missing can of soup. Suddenly, a stranger enters the darkened room and a fight breaks out. It turns out to be Barry King, who bites Sam, takes their picture, and accuses them of robbery and murder. Down at police headquarters, Sam and Honey explain to the lieutenant that they were hired by Corbin and that King, in Sam's words, "is just a two-bit press agent–he's trying to get a good story." As the three men argue, Honey takes the soup can and opens it. Out pours chicken noodle soup–when the can in question was chicken gumbo. The lieutenant subsequently dismisses Sam and Honey, declaring, "What this case needs is a chef!"

Back at the office, the duo debates the various modus operandi of the soup thief. They conclude that the man who hired the thief subsequently killed him and still has the original can. They decide to pay Corbin's studio a final visit and, while prowling around in the dark, express disbelief over his seemingly absurd and ultra-expensive pop art. Honey decides to search upstairs, where she finds the genuine article in the cupboard. "It was just waiting for old Mother Hubbard!" she notes. Suddenly, the lights go on and Mr. Van Wyck holds her at gunpoint. He then convinces Sam to drop his gun and takes them to a hidden art vault behind the curtain. Here Van Wyck keeps his personal art collection, a very expensive mélange of stolen masterpieces. From his gleeful giddiness, they can detect he is a true art connoisseur. "What's a highbrow like you doing selling pop art?" Sam asks. "For the money, of course. There's a fortune in pop art," Van Wyck says. "We highbrows have to eat too, you know." Van Wyck then locks the two in the art vault, assuring them that although they will have suffocated by the time he gets back from Europe, they will perish surrounded by artistic splendor. The villain then shuts off their air supply, giving the duo 20 minutes to come up with something. Honey then gets on her microphone and alerts Van Wyck that Sam is going crazy and destroying his art collection through sheer clumsiness. He can hear crashing and tearing noises over the transceiver. Alarmed for his collection, Van Wyck reopens the vault and fires at a flashlight placed on a stand. The two jump on him from the corners, overcoming and knocking him against a display with angel wings. As Van Wyck hangs there, centered between the two wings, Sam says, "You know something, that's pretty artistic–we ought to name it!" "Let's call it 'Jail Bird,'" Honey laughs. That night Sam, Honey, Meg, and Corbin are at dinner for a celebration and the artist toasts Honey for "getting me out of the soup." The waiter then appears and inquires if they wish to have soup or salad with their dinner. "Salad!" is the unanimous response.

"Little Green Robin Hood"

(Aired March 18, 1966)

Starring: Edd Byrnes (Robin Hood), Severn Darden (Dr. Gregory Ames), Francois Ruggeri (Annette), Allen Jenkins (Max), Peter Leeds (Lieutenant), Eleanor Audrey (Mrs. Carleton Murdock).

Script: Ken Kolb

Directed by: Sidney Miller

Honey and Sam drive up to exclusive Sherwood Park, a wealthy, gated community, and they are closely grilled by Max the security guard. They all know each other but a recent rash of jewels thefts at Sherwood forces Max to check everybody's credentials to keep the undesirables out. "I'm really head of the mob–but I had a facelift," Sam tells him. "You should get your money back!" Max counters. "If we find the burglar, Max, we'll tell him to stop by and sign in," Honey chides. The duo stops at the home of Mrs. Carleton Murdock, who has hired them to solve the recent thievery. En route, Honey espies a man moving through the bushes in distinctly medieval attire. She roars after him in pursuit, but he ducks into the bushes and fires an arrow at her car, puncturing the tire. Honey screeches off the road and skids to a halt. The arrow is retrieved and has a note attached reading, "The protector of Sherwood Forest bids you welcome–Robin Hood." They then relate the information to Mrs. Murdock, who is incredulous and berates them for being ridiculous. "You don't think we'd make a thing like that up?" Sam growls. "You know–that's the only thing in your favor," Mrs. Murdock sneers, "It's so completely outrageous, I suppose it must be the truth!"

The discussion is interrupted by Murdock's comely French maid Annette, who announces that Dr. Ames has arrived. She ogles Sam for a second, then goes off to fetch Dr. Ames, a somewhat smug psychologist and neighbor of Mrs. Murdock. Honey informs him that the suspect is Robin Hood, to which Ames, pouring himself a drink, sneers, "Everyone's making it on pills nowadays — I'm old fashioned, I stick to gin." As Honey and Sam depart, Ames taunts them with, "My best to Robin Hood!" Honey reacts fiercely to the remark and strides over to return fire when Sam grabs and pulls her along. Back outside, they begin searching for the culprit in the adjoining woods. At length "Robin" finds them across a stream and challenges Sam, whom he regards as Little John, to a fight with quarterstaffs in midstream. Honey, sympathetically encourages Sam to humor him and the two fight on a log to a draw, falling in the water. Robin then befriends Honey, who introduces herself as Maid Marian and starts probing where his hideout is. Resenting the intrusion, Robin asks, "Why does Robin Hood steal from the rich?" "Because the poor have bad jewelry?" Honey replies. Robin promises to show them his lair, but only after they demonstrate their loyalty by stealing a piece of valuable jewelry from the rich and bringing it to him. "Well, Maid Marian, what doeth we do now?" Sam inquires. "We become one of Robin's hoods," she responds. Back at the house, Sam and Honey request that Mrs. Murdock lend them a little something–her emerald necklace. "A little something?!" she recoils in amazement, "Robin Hood's dementia seems to be contagious!" Dr. Ames agrees and cautions against trying to fool Robin with phony stones. Nonetheless, an incredulous Murdock surrenders her necklace to the investigators.

Honey next meets Robin alone in the woods, gives him the necklace, all the while pressing him for the location of his lair. He refuses to show it outright, but he gives her a hint that it is surrounded by "currant" vines. Before he departs, Honey hands him a transmitter ring and ask that he carry it always. Robin smiles, kisses her, and agrees. Moments later, Sam is tracking Robin with an electronic device. They subsequently find him lying dead in a copse—shot by an arrow—and the necklace is missing. That evening Sam and Honey have an impossible time explaining to the police they have been pursuing a thief who thinks he is Robin Hood. The lieutenant rolls up his eyes in disbelief, uttering, "Oh, boy, my mother wanted me to be a violinist—but, no, I had to be a cop!" The lieutenant then asks Dr. Ames if he thinks the victim was Robin Hood. "No ... but I think that he thought so," Ames dryly intones. Some sarcastic bantering follows, then the lieutenant is grateful just to send for the coroner's office and leave. Mrs. Murdock, however, is outraged by the loss of her expensive necklace and warns that if the duo do not produce it within 24 hours, her attorney is going to sue them. She then orders Annette to escort them out the back door. As the comely maid continues eyeing Sam, Honey advises, "Don't waste your charms on him—he's practically a convict!" The duo begins combing through the woods and Honey suddenly reinterprets the clue as "current" as in electric–and that Robin's lair is probably a utility service tunnel. The two eventually stumble upon it. "I hope this is Robin's hideout," a weary Sam declares. "If it isn't, it may have to be ours," Honey counters. The jewels, however, are missing save for a single cufflink, and it dawns on Sam that Dr. Ames was the only other person that knew about the jewels. Back at the house, Ames and Annette are preparing to haul their valuable stash off to Switzerland. Suddenly, the door opens as Sam and Honey confront the two head-on. "Is archery your hobby, doctor?" she asks as a fight ensues. The criminals are subdued and Honey finds the missing emerald necklace. Sam congratulates her but she remains a little dejected. "Poor Robin, he'll never forgive us," she insists. "We have to give it back to the rich."

"Just the Bear Facts, Ma'am"

(Aired March 25, 1966)

Starring: Richard Carlyle (Twily), Frank Wilcox (Mr. Burgess), Frank Gerstyle (director), Mousie Garner (Igor), Marvin Brody (bear trainer), Lonie Fotre (Miss Dawn), Robert Kenneally (Mr. Hero), Don Gazzaniga (Jago).

Script: Gwen Bagni, Paul Dubov

Directed by: James Brown

The scene opens in a darkened castle, thunder and lightening pealing in the background. Honey lies crouching in a corner as a mad henchman, Igor, declares that if he cannot have her, no one will. He then releases an angry bear that chases Honey around while an earthquake begins shaking the building. A falling beam knocks Honey flat when, suddenly, a hero appears who shoots Igor and the bear dead, then gently cradles her in his arms, cooing, "Darling, I'm sorry." A director then yells, "Cut!" strolls over, and congratulates Honey for a job well done. Dusting herself off, she tells him, "When you hired me to double as a movie star I had visions of grandeur." However, Honey has been hired to investigate the mysterious death of a stunt girl killed performing the same act. Honey cannot see how it was anything if not an accident, but Mr. Burgess informs her that he received a mysterious phone call calling him to the set – and when he arrived she was dead. "She was one of the finest stunt girls in the business. That's what bothers me–being killed in such a simple stunt–just a beam falling." Outside, filming continues with a mad bear knocking cowboys around. The director yells, "Cut!"– the bear takes off his mask to reveal Sam Bolt masquerading as an animal actor. Honey calls him over, noting, "No matter what anybody says, you're this Honey's bear." Sam, shaking his head, groans, "Oh, brother..." He then informs her that everybody on the set thinks the stunt girl's death was accidental. Their attention is broken by a vocal dispute between Jago, the stunt coordinator, and Twily, the prop man. Jago is livid that Twily could think any of his stunts are not safe and Twily declares his only concern is for the new stunt girl. The unit director arrives to break up the dispute, and the two part. Honey, meanwhile, has a fight scene coming up so she drops by Twily's office for her stunt pads. He redirects her over to Jago's department and, while departing, she marvels over all the valuable-looking items—especially an exquisite, old clock. Twily smiles and explains they are fake, all being made at the studio.

Back on the street, Honey doubles for a Wild West heroine, is picked up by the leading man–then unceremoniously dropped in the mud. Sam graciously helps her out of the puddle, expressing concern over the hanging scene that is coming up. "Sam, you worry too much," she says. To quell his fears, Honey shows how safe the noose is by putting her neck inside–but the trap door mysteriously opens and Sam catches her at the last second. That evening, Sam and Honey are waiting for the studio crew to depart so they can investigate the editing room. Reviewing the facts, he insists that someone is trying to kill Honey. "Perils of Pauline you're not," he snarls. Still, Honey has a hunch and, once before the editing machine, she insists on comparing her dungeon scene with that of the deceased stunt girl. The two scenes are nearly identical until the beam falls–directly on the girl. "She missed her mark," Sam says, "it was an accident." Honey, however, insists that the beam is falling differently–the stunt was rigged for murder. The duo goes to the soundstage and checks the chandelier, which appears safely secured. Sam then wanders off briefly while Honey lies down and closes her eyes. In her reverie she sees a continuous montage of herself and Sam in numerous old films, yet an old-fashioned clock motif somehow keeps appearing at inopportune times.

Once awakened, it suddenly dawns on Honey that the film sequences they observed differed because the one with the stunt girl has a rich clock in it–the same one she saw at Twily's prop room. It suddenly dawns on her that Honey's predecessor was an antique specialist who recognized the prop as a precious item–and was killed for it. When Honey also noted the clock for what it was, Twily tried to silence her as well. The duo rush over to the prop room where Twily and two assistants are loading valuable antiques onto a lunch wagon. "It's a little late, but something's cooking," Honey whispers. The three men split up to round up valuables from various places and Sam and Honey decide to move in and end their little charade. Honey enters the prop room, where Twily is moving a clock, and informs him, "Twily, your time is up." He resists and, a few chops later, lays prostrate on the floor beneath a dummy strung up by a noose. "Hang around with your friend," she murmurs, "we'll be back." Meanwhile, Sam is cleaning up the other two hoods while Honey chases and dispatches a third. The two gumshoes then confront each other in a mock street fight before she goes, "Let's wrap it up and call the law!" The next day a dapper Mr. Burgess heartily thanks Honey for her help and mentions his constant need to discover new faces. She is quite flattered that he likes her acting and coyly inquires if a contract is in the offing. "That is exactly what I am talking about, Miss West," Burgess enthusiastically agrees, "because, I tell you, Sam Bolt is the greatest bear personality the screen has ever discovered!" Sam steps out of a nearby dressing room, resplendent in his bear outfit, and agrees with Burgess's assessment that he "is marvelous." Somewhat deflated, Honey pulls the bear mask over Sam's face, declaring, "Don't lose your head!"

"There's a Long, Long Fuse a' Burning"

(Aired April 1, 1966)

Starring: Dick Clark (Peyton), Paul Dubov (Lieutenant Badger), John Holland (Piccadilly Charlie), David Fresco (Mousey), Richard Hoyt (drunk), Lennie Bremen (Maxie Bripp).

Script: Gwen Bagni, Paul Dubov

Directed by: Thomas Carr

In a seedy penny arcade, Honey West is shadowing Mousey, an older man suspected of planting bombs to rob banks. She contacts Sam on her powder case microphone, disbelieving that an old man would do such a thing. "Tell that to the jury that convicted him," he reminds her. Suddenly, a drunken patron forces a stuffed animal on her and she hastily relocates to another part of the room. Honey tries contacting Sam again by microphone, but he doesn't respond. In fact, two thugs have jumped Sam in the alley and are working him over. Honey runs over to help and the punks flee, then Sam groggily exclaims, "Hey, that's great—I get slugged and you win a kewpie doll!" He takes Honey's stuffed dog and tosses it in a trash can–where it promptly explodes. "A kewpie doll bomb!" he explains. "What did you win?" "My next birthday," she replies. The duo are next at police headquarters looking at mug shots and an incredulous Lieutenant Badger refuses to believe their story. He also berates their latest client, ex-felon bomber Maxie Bripp, Mousey's former employer and who is also a prime suspect in a recent rash of bank bombings and robberies. Honey and Sam pay a visit to Maxie, who stridently denies any knowledge of the crimes. In fact, Maxie is proud of the fact he has been rehabilitated and is now a wealthy philanthropist. Moreover, Mousey has also changed and is, in Maxie's words, "true blue." "Perhaps he changed his colors," Sam notes. "Like green as in money," Honey interjects. Growing increasingly annoyed at these proceedings is Peyton, Maxie's imperious publicity agent, who reminds him that other clients are waiting. "One other thing, Mr. Bripp," he sneers, "please stop pacing as if you're still living in a cell." Once Peyton departs, Bripp explains that he built and runs the Bastille Club to keep former cons off the street–including his three former gang members. "I keep these ex-cons off the relief rolls and a return to a life of crime," he moans. "Why do they persecute me?" Maxie also feels that the culprits who copied his style of bank robbery are hard at work as they speak.

A rash of explosions/robberies is then committed by a gang wearing rubber masks and white wigs. Maxie, again a prime suspect, is jailed by the police after they searched his office and found a rubber mask which he kept for "sentimental reasons." Sam and Honey visit him to arrange bail but Maxie refuses, noting that the next time the bandits strike, he will be behind bars with a ready-made alibi in hand. Peyton also visits his cell and Maxie berates him for being late. Peyton claims to have been engaged with other business and Maxie pulls a long blonde hair off his jacket, "Blonde business?" Sam and Honey depart to find a note in their van telling them to wait in a darkened alley at night. They park exactly as instructed, although Honey cannot open the door owing to a pile of garbage cans and asks Sam to pull up some. Suddenly, the garbage cans explode–a failed assassination attempt. The next day, the duo pulls up in front of the exclusive Bastille Club, and have trouble getting in past a snooty doorman. After formally introducing themselves, he smiles and allows them in-even though the club does not allow women. The doorman also declares that he is formally known as "Piccadilly Charlie," a former cat burglar, now gone straight thanks to Maxie. Sam and Honey are subsequently introduced to Maxie's old gang, now a bunch of tottering old men. Mousey explains that they would never hurt people and, even in their prime, they only carried fake guns. Charlie orders coffee for his two guests–then Honey recognizes the waiter as the man who forced the kewpie doll bomb on her. He flees the building and makes his escape before Honey can catch up.

Sam thinks that the old men are still in the business somehow, but Honey has her doubts, given the youthful thugs that bounced him. They also wonder who could have possibly known that Maxie was in prison–other than Peyton. Sam and Honey then explain to an irate Lieutenant Badger that they want to vacuum Maxie's cell for "sanitary" reasons. Actually, Honey wants to "split a blonde hair" by retrieving the strand pulled earlier from Peyton's jacket. Once recovered and tested, it turns out to have come from a wig. As they speak, Peyton and his gang are planning their latest heist when Maxie calls from his cell and wants to see him. Peyton excuses himself for the evening—business, he claims—while Sam and Honey listen in. They then trail the hoods to the Apex Company and watch them set off a bomb to distract the guard and enter while he is not looking. Sam and Honey intend to catch them in the act of opening the safe and tell Maxie to remain in the van. However, they are captured at gunpoint by Peyton, who ties them up and places a small incendiary bomb at their feet. "Bad public relations," Honey declares. Suddenly, Maxie shows up behind the wall, pulls a knife from Sam's pocket, and cuts them free. The thieves depart hurriedly with the loot, then Sam chases them outside and stuns them with their own fire bomb. He and Honey quickly subdue them, then she asks Maxie how he managed to get past the guard. "Very easy," Maxie says with a grin. "This is the Apex Company, ain't it? I just told him I was Mr. Apex!" The next evening Sam and Honey are hosted and toasted at the Bastille Club, and she becomes "the only female of the species" granted honorary membership.

"An Eerie, Airy Thing"

(Aired April 8, 1966)

Starring: Lisa Seagram (Connie Philips), Adam Williams (Gordon Forbes), Lou Krugman, (Stuart Bell), Bill Quinn (Lieutenant Curtis), Ken Lynch (Lieutenant Barney), Jan Arvan (Mrs. Ruth), Michael Harris (technician).

Script: William Link, Richard Levinson

Directed by: James Brown

An anxious crowd gathers below a high-rise building where, above them, Gordon Forbes perches on a ledge, apparently waiting to jump. Sam Bolt is leaning outside a nearby window and appealing to Forbes, an old Marine Corps buddy, to come inside. Apparently, he telephoned Sam to his room for consolation–then went on the ledge. Forbes refuses to comply–until he can speak with his wife Diana, who tossed him out because of gambling debts from the Sunset Club. Meanwhile, Honey West enters the room and confers with Sam. They are interrupted by Mr. Rush, the hotel manager, who mentions he grew suspicious when Forbes rented the room without bringing any luggage. Repeated phone calls to the Forbes residence go unanswered, so Honey volunteers to find Diana herself. However, as she pulls in the driveway, two shots ring out. Honey bolts inside to find Diana dead on the floor, just as a car peals out of the driveway. The police arrive and Lieutenant Curtis grills Honey, who cannot supply them with any details. "Talk about a brick wall," Curtis bemoans. "The man won't come in unless we bring him his wife–and now his wife is dead!" Honey calls Sam to inform him that Diana was murdered–and they do not dare tell Forbes. She next decides to investigate matters at the Sunset Club for possible leads.

Once inside, Honey goes to see Stuart Bell, a former con, whom she had previously helped convict, but who has since mended his ways. "I am going straight now–I'm growing conservative in my old age," he assures her. Despite a friendly exchange, Honey reminds Bell that he runs a clandestine gambling operation on the second floor of his health club–and wants answers. To begin with, how much does Forbes owe him? Bell hesitates, then mentions $20,000. Honey postulates that if Diana Forbes had a large life-insurance policy, her death would handily provide her husband, as beneficiary, sufficient funding to retire all his debts. Bell insists he did not do it and, in fact, he met Forbes's wife recently and liked her. "Good-looking woman–if you like brunette," Bell hints. "Maybe you've been able to help me after all," Honey declares. "Diana Forbes is a blonde!" Honey next enters the advertising office of Gordon Forbes and begins rummaging through his papers. Informing Sam of her discoveries, he mutters, "Breaking and entering ..."— then faintly recognizes the woman in question. At this juncture, Lieutenant Wyman suggests lowering a man on a rope and grabbing Forbes before he can jump–exactly what Mr. Rush has in mind. "There's got to be a better way," Sam states. "Then we'd better invent one and soon," Barney warns." He's getting impatient." Before leaving, Rush mentions that he has also seen the woman and, in a flash, Sam recognizes her as a television personality. Sam and Honey rush outside and approach a TV technician with the photo of the mystery woman. He instantly recognizes her as Connie Phillips, a local weather girl on another station. Sam then goes back upstairs. "I'll try to catch the weather lady during commercials," Honey blurts. She enters the studio as Connie is giving her report, then approaches her for information. "Show's over, friend, I'm in a hurry," she replies, until Honey displays the photograph. Connie, crestfallen, then admits she and Gordon had an affair which ended the week previously. She is also shocked to learn that Diana Forbes was murdered. However, Connie still refuses to help Gordon out of fear of getting fired. "Sorry, Gordon is not my problem anymore," she insists. Honey intends to inform the police, then Connie suddenly changes her tune and agrees to cooperate. However, back in her dressing room, she phones the front desk and has them page Honey West. Honey walks over to a phone, realizes that she has been duped, and races back to find Connie gone. She calls Sam and informs her that the suspect lives at 596 Ventura and tells him to meet her there. Sam arrives and catches Connie in the act of packing. Connie plays coy for a few seconds and again complains that she might lose her job if word of her affair reaches the newspapers. Connie then pulls a gun and escapes out the door. Suddenly, a loud thump resonates from outside and Connie comes flying back in-with Honey standing triumphantly over her. "I think the forecast for you is a little stormy," Sam informs her. Honey, examining Connie's gun, notes that it has been fired four times-yet Diana was shot only twice. The duo take Diana back to the hotel room. Honey then gets permission from Lieutenant Barney to talk to Gordon–and she promptly informs him that his wife is dead. "Get her away from there," Barney angrily states. "Lieutenant, he's not going to jump-he never intended to," Honey informs him. "This whole thing was a set-up." Honey informs Gordon how he killed his wife with two bullets, then had Connie fire two more bullets once somebody drove up in the driveway. Moreover, Connie is now in the room behind them. "You've got two choices-the pavement or the jury," Honey slyly declares. "At least with the jury you've got a chance." Gordon realizes that the game is up and comes off the ledge. Sam and Honey are relieved that the matter has been resolved and she wants some champagne. Sam suggests dinner at an exclusive Roof Top Room on the top of the building. Honey, however, has had enough of heights for the day–and insists on going to Luigi's Cellar. Sam, resigned to his fate, simply complies.

Appendix

The ABC Television Network Presents "Interview Specials" with the Stars of *Honey West*. ABC Records #865-USA
Dick Stroud, Hollywood Commentator. Cut #1–Anne Francis.

DS: A swinging male-female team of private eyes hits the TV tube Friday nights when ABC Television launches its exciting new *Honey West* series. In the title role of the new show will be lovely Anne Francis. We are very fortunate to have Anne on our direct line to Television Center today and we're going to have her tell us all about Honey. Anne, we're delighted to have you here.

Anne: Well, thank you, it's very nice to be here.

DS: *Honey West* series is going to be something really different with you and John Ericson in the co-starring role as a way-out private-eye team, and your relationship will be a fascinating one to say the least. Could you tell us about it?

Anne: We have what you could call a loving animosity and almost every show we run into a battle. We battle each other, but we protect each other against everyone else.

DS: And some of your adversaries are going to have plenty of evil potential from what I hear. You had to climb down the side of a building, they tell me, to make an escape in one of the episodes.

Anne: Yes, on the pilot of the film, I had to do some rope work. Naturally, we had a wonderful stunt gal who really did the work from thirteen stories up at the Continental Hotel, but I did my own rope work in the studio from the catwalk up above, which is about 25-30 feet, hand over hand.

DS: So, sounds like a strenuous show.

Anne: It's a pretty strenuous show; we also have karate and jujitsu battles in almost every show.

DS: They tell me you're pretty proficient in these, if you'll excuse the expression, manly arts. I mean judo and karate.

Anne: Why, I studied for a number weeks before I did *Burke's Law*—on *Burke's Law* they introduced Honey West—and I worked with a most marvelous instructor who teaches Okinawa Tae, and it's a very beautiful form of karate. It's much like body fencing and it's strenuous as ballet is strenuous.

DS: How would you explain the character of Honey West? She's certainly unique.

Anne: Well, to explain Honey is that she's a modern-day Perils of Pauline or Pearl White.

DS: What's her personality like?

Anne: She finds life a great challenge; she likes to know how people are put together and why. She's quite a psychologist. She uses her feminine instincts in whatever situation she finds herself. If she's talking to a lady suspect, she becomes one of the girls. If she's talking to a gentleman suspect, she's sizes him up as, well, what way to approach him.

DS: In other words, she's called upon to use her wiles as well as her wits. What sort of wardrobe will she have, any particular costume?

Anne: All of her clothes will be glamorous for the most part, and of course, she will go into disguises. She carries a jeweled gun. She has two jeweled guns, as a matter of act. She has a Derringer for her party purse and then she has the .38 for more serious work.

DS: I'd hate to be the object of any of her more serious work. As a suspense, mystery-comedy, the *Honey West* series is going to allow full play for your versatility. It ought to be fun.

Anne: John Ericson and I also have the fun of being able to use disguises and different dialects and such, so there are many different directions we can go in.

DS: With all her prowess in karate and judo, and her ability to scale walls and give her male partner a battle now and then, Honey West is still going to be kept quite feminine, isn't she?

Anne: Quite feminine. I am luxuriating in furs and jewels and beautiful gowns and such that I love - any girl would.

DS: What's Honey West's background in the series? How did she hook up with Sam Bolt, the partner who's played by

	John Ericson? And how did she become a private eye?
Anne:	My father–Honey's father–was a private investigator. At the time of his death, Sam took over with Honey as partners.
DS:	Much of Sam Bolt's time, I understand, is taken up trying to keep Honey out of dangerous situations. How does she get into them in the first place?
Anne:	She gets—just sorta gets—involved in dangerous situations, not always deliberately, but it just seems to happen. As much as Sam tries to keep her out of it, she seems to be in the midst of it.
DS:	Well, Anne, you're coming into the *Honey West* series with a rich background of experience as a television actress. Tell me, is a person like yourself able to sit back and enjoy a television show when you see one at home, or are you critical of the technical aspects?
Anne:	You reach a point where you can see the technical aspects and still enjoy the performance.
DS:	Well, we're certainly going to look forward to your performances, along with your co-star John Ericson, and what promises to be a great hit television series *Honey West*, Fridays, ABC Television Network. We want to thank you very much for sharing your time with us, Anne Francis, we're certain our audience enjoyed it tremendously as we did.
Anne:	Thank you so much, I enjoyed it too.
DS:	Dick Strout reporting from Television Center in Hollywood, returning to our main studios.

Appendix

The ABC Television Network Presents "Interview Specials" with the Stars of *Honey West*.
Dick Strout, Hollywood Commentator.
Cut # 2–John Ericson ABC-865-USA

DS: Another in the great array of new television shows ABC has lined up for us this fall is *Honey West*, starring John Ericson and Anne Francis. We interviewed Ericson on the Hollywood set of *Honey West* and he filled us in on what promises to be a terrifically exciting new series with John as Sam Bolt and Anne Francis in the key role as Honey West. They're a couple of private eyes with a very interesting relationship. Ericson explains it.

John: They fight together all the time, they tell each other what to do all the time, one resists the other's opinion all the time. This is what gets them into all kinds of scraps all the time and all the unique situations we get into.

DS: *Honey West*, which hits the air at 9 o'clock on Friday nights over ABC, is a suspense/ mystery/comedy in which John Ericson plays a bombastic Sam Bolt.

John: I would say he's more or less very serious/surly; he's got a sense of humor, but he flies off the handle very easily, especially when he has to deal with Honey's intuition as far as certain things are concerned. Sam Bolt believes that the only way to deal in detective work is through facts, and Honey West believes woman's intuition takes care of a lot of things. This is one big point, that I get very angry about it.

DS: *Honey West* is unique as a series in that Anne Francis in the title role and John Ericson as Sam Bolt play a male/female private-eye team.

John: It slants towards the boy/girl James Bond—that's what we are, actually.

DS: But in terms of unusual weaponry and strange detection devices, the Honey West series bids fair to outdo even the dauntless 007.

John: We'll have weird weapons, strange weapons, things that you've never heard of or audiences have never seen before. We'll have radio transistors in watches and cigarette packs and fountain pens. We'll have spying equipment coming out of flower delivery trucks or TV repair trucks. We'll have television sets that spy on you; they take your picture as you're watching it. We'll have light bulbs that record you or take your picture, or we'll have pictures on walls with the face of the person in the eye of the camera. We'll have all kinds of strange, strange, weird things.

DS: At just about that point in my interview with John Ericson, we were interrupted by a business-like assistant director.

John: Do you hear that? That means they need me on the set for a minute.

DS: And off he went to shoot a scene in which he desperately tried to keep Honey West from getting into a tangle with an evildoer who is a karate expert. I won't tell you who won but when Sam Bolt came back to our microphone I asked him if he often succeeded in keeping the heroine out of trouble.

John: No, I don't succeed in keeping her out of trouble because she insists on getting into trouble, and I have to

	come and bail her out all the time. I have to be the cavalry, you know, with trumpets blaring.
DS:	Maybe you're wondering if there's a romance between Bolt and Honey West, or if it's strictly a platonic relationship. Well, Ericson wouldn't tell.
John:	No, that's a secret and that's something we'd like the audience to read into the series. Sam Bolt and Honey West have known each other for many, many years and, as a matter of fact, they even went back to childhood together. And when they decided to go into business together and become partners, they find it works out very well. They both like high adventure and they both like crazy sports cars, they like crazy pets like the ocelot, you know, it's lots of fun, it's two companions going through life doing the same thing.
DS:	I asked where in a continuing series such as *Honey West* if there was an opportunity for ad-libbing or whether the actors were required to stick rigidly to the script.
John:	No, we have no ad-libbing, especially if you're doing a running character. Annie and I will know our director so well by the time that we get halfway through the show that many times things will happen on the set and we'll say things on the screen, and it will remain in the script as part of the character.
DS:	*Honey West*, of course, was the central character in the original novel on which the ABC Television series was based. Sam Bolt is new on the scene. He wasn't in that first book.
John:	No, he was not in the book, there was a character in

the book called Johnny Dark, but he was not associated with Honey, he just ran in and out as one of her boyfriends. Now, the new novels they're writing, they're including Sam Bolt.

DS: So you'll be able not only see him but you can read about him in all the forthcoming novels. Well, just at that point in the interview the director called John Ericson back to shoot another scene in the *Honey West* episode. I strongly recommend that you catch this series, it's something excitingly new in television. *Honey West*, co-starring Anne Francis and John Ericson, Friday nights at nine on the ABC Television Network. This is Dick Strout reporting from Television Center in Hollywood, returning you to our main studios.

Footnotes

1. Joel Sternberg. "Honey West." In: *Encyclopedia of Television*, 2nd Edition. Edited by Horace Newcomb. 3 Vols. New York, Fitzroy Dearborn, 2004, Vol. 2, 1125. The distinction should be made that Honey West was not the first televised female detective, only the first to operate her own agency. In contrast, early female dicks on the tube were invariably cast as sidekicks or secondary characters in a series. The overall novelty of *Honey West* has also failed to produce a body of scholarly literature expounding on it; the only detailed treatment remains Julie D'Acci. "Nobody's Woman? Honey West and the New Sexuality." In: *The Revolution Wasn't Televised: Sixties Television and Social Conflict*. Edited by Lynn Spiegel and Michael Curtin. New York: Routledge, 1997, 73-94. This erudite piece leans heavily on sociological discourse and is really less about the TV show than the context of its times.

2. In the words of one authority, "Spelling's genius had always been to spot a trend and refashion it with an original twist...It was Spelling who envisioned a character more aligned with Bond girls than with Cricket or the girlfriends at Sunset Strip." Linda Mizejewski. *Hardboiled & High Heeled: The Woman Detective in Popular Culture*. New York: Routledge, 2004, 55.

3. Aaron Spelling. *A Prime-Time Life*. New York: St. Martin's Press, 1996, 54.

4. However, the opening credits to *Honey West* remain a model of titil-

lation and sexual suggestiveness. "An extreme close-up of her lips, slyly open and accompanied by a beauty mark, is followed by a shot of her looking out at the camera from behind sunglasses, then a sequence juxtaposing a man's ear with her mouth. Several action stills reveal her evening gown, cleavage, and revolver, all equally at the ready." Toby Miller. *Spyscreen: Espionage on Film and TV from the 1930s to the 1960s*. New York: Oxford University Press, 2003, 162.

5. One scholar of the genre opines that "The female detective on television is often bracketed by male detectives and not allowed to investigate independently...Thus Honey West pairs Honey with a male partner who does not exist in the series of books upon which the show is based." Lisa M. Dresner. *The Female Investigator in Literature, Film, and Popular Culture*. Jefferson, N.C.: McFarland, 2007, 68. This is a misnomer with no basis in fact; it was Honey's over-reliance on intuition and persistent penchant for charging off on her own that sparked the many conflicts with an overprotective Sam Bolt. As an ace private investigator, nobody "bracketed" Honey West under any circumstances.

6. Mizejewski, *Hardboiled & High Heeled*, 59. The author continues: "True, the *Honey West* episodes were fairly predictable in their plot-lines and not especially well-written. When Emma Peel arrived in a funnier and wittier British version of the female spy, she had a far happier life on prime time." *Ibid*, 57. Another equally uncharitable assessment was proffered by Jon E. Lewis and Penny Stempel: "Intended to be noteworthy for its gutsy heroine, it was in fact mostly memorable for the fight scenes in which a man with a blonde wig was quite obviously wheeled in to do the stunts." John E. Lewis and Penny Stempel. *Cult TV: The Essential Critical Guide*. London: Pavillion, 1993, 79.

7. "Recently watching a sampling of *Honey West* episodes, I remembered my 1965 junior-high school adulation of this series....in this pre-Avengers era, Honey West was the only grown-up woman on television with an interesting life." Mizejewski, *Hardboiled & High Heeled*, 58. On a more visceral level, film writer Laura Wagner concedes,

"There was something empowering about a karate-chopping female private eye who could duke it out with the big boys and win." Laura Wagner, "Private Eyeful: Honey West Revisited," *Classic Images* No. 400 (October 2008), 6. This popular piece is required reading for all *Honey West* fans for the writer displays an astonishing grasp of her subject matter, lucidly presented.

8. An enthusiastic review of the DVD series by David J. Hogan is in *Filmfax Plus* No. 119 (Winter 2008): 18-20.

www.ingramcontent.com/pod-product-compliance
Lightning Source LLC
Chambersburg PA
CBHW071436150426
43191CB00008B/1148